Fourth Edition

Mystery Shopping

GET PAID TO SHOP

JIM POYNTER

Leromi Publishing

First edition 1996
Fourth Edition 2002

Printed and bound in the United States of America.

ISBN 0-9713585-4-0

Library of Congress Control Number: 2001095635

Library of Congress
Cataloging-in-Publication Data

Poynter, James M.
Mystery shopping / Jim Poynter. — 4th ed.
p. cm.
Includes index.

1. Personal shoppers. I. Title

TX335.P67 2002 640'.73
QBI01-201254

Leromi Publishing
PO Box 40484
Denver, Colorado 80204
www.mysteryshoppingbook.net

Printed in the United States of America
10 9 8 7 6 5 4 3 2 1

CONTENTS

Acknowledgments

Few books are the work of only the author. This one is certainly no exception. Many have contributed. Special thanks go to Howard Troxell, co-owner of J&K Shopping Service, Inc. and the National Shopping Service Network in Denver. Howard not only gave me my first job as a mystery shopper, but he has been a source of mystery shopping information and inspiration ever since. Howard's partner, Jerry Goodwin, has also been of considerable assistance. Most of the forms reproduced in this book (with their permission) originated with one or both of the mystery shopping companies headed up by Howard and Jerry.

Thanks go to Irving Ehudin, formerly with the Merit Service Division of Borg Warner Information Services, Inc. He provided knowledge and information on embezzlement reduction mystery shopping and security mystery shopping.

Many people provided information on techniques used in applying mystery shopping approaches and the screening of potential mystery shoppers. Thanks for information and help in these areas go to Helen Robin, with Dale Systems, Inc. in Garden City, New York;

Celine Estile, with ADB in Cincinnati; Marie Brady, formerly with Confero Inc. in Cary, North Carolina; Sharon Sparks, with Gray Mark Security Group in Plantation, Florida; and Bonnie Conner, with Quality Assessments Mystery Shoppers in Austin, Texas.

Thanks also go to Donna Hargrave of Houston. Donna was the first of several people who provided information on how to start a local mystery shopping service on a shoestring. Even though others have followed in her footsteps, few have been able to do it (succeed) with so few up-front dollars.

To the people who have taken my seminars on Mystery Shopping and then stayed in touch and contributed—sometimes substantially—to my knowledge, my newsletter, and this book, I offer my thanks. They are among the most important source of continuing knowledge regarding the job of mystery shopping. Premier among these and thanked from the bottom of my heart is Anne Marie Gunther. Every few weeks, she leaves a message on my voice mail or sends me an envelope of information. An active mystery shopper, Anne Marie can be counted on to stay abreast of everything that is new in mystery shopping—and I thank her for keeping me up-to-date as well.

Caroline Ghanbari is another previous student who keeps me advised of what is happening in her world of mystery shopping. I am grateful for these and other past students who periodically send me their success stories and informative tidbits. Perhaps more than anything else an author and a lecturer appreciates hearing from those who used his information to become successful.

Thanks also go to educator and associate, Brian

Garrity. He made excellent suggestions regarding information organization and the flow/structure of chapters in the book.

Those involved in the book production, manufacturing, and marketing processes have helped to make this a sellout with each edition. Many people consider my cousin, Dan Poynter, to be the guru of self-publishing, and I thank him for recommending several of the individuals who have contributed to the processes that turned raw manuscript into a quality book.

All illustrations were prepared by Allan Guth. His tireless work with the author to get each detail just right is much appreciated. His work on the cover drawing was especially difficult and demanding.

Simon Warwick and Patty Vadinsky of Warwick Associates contributed, and continue to contribute, the many small touches that make the difference between a quality publication and one that is just average. Patty was instrumental in providing a menu of changes to facilitate marketing to major buying groups such as libraries, catalogs, and retail bookstores. She and Simon offer steady help in reaching the book and consumer press media with promotions targeted to their needs.

Robert Howard is considered one of the top book cover design specialists in the country. His work with the cover of the fourth edition of *Mystery Shopping* has contributed substantially to the overall professional image of the book. It is a privilege to be able to draw upon his years of experience in cover design for the current edition.

The Roberts Group provided book typesetting, forms development, and indexing. They, too, are considered to be among the best in their field. While the average reader expects no more than a smooth-flowing book, The Roberts Group have made the book admired by even the professionals in the book production industry. They are thanked for going far beyond what one would expect from book production experts.

Thank you to those who sponsor my continuing education seminars in cities throughout the country and allow me to spread the mystery shopping "gospel" through the vehicle of seminar presentations. I am especially grateful to John Hand, owner and director of Denver-based Colorado Free University. John told others that mystery shopping is the current "hot topic" and thereby encouraged many continuing education center directors to schedule seminars on mystery shopping.

Also especially thanked is Ted Weisgal, co-founder and co-director of Leisure Learning Unlimited, Inc. in Houston. Addressing a large gathering of continuing education directors, Ted spoke with wild enthusiasm on behalf of Mystery Shopping as a seminar (and Jim Poynter as its presenter).

Thank you to other directors as well: Bill Hogue, with FunEd in Dallas; Carol Petrocelli, formerly with the Learning Exchange in Weathersby, Connecticut; Dina Grumann, former owner of Bay Winds in Tampa; Rebecca Zeiler, with the Boulder Valley School District in Boulder, Colorado; Gretchen Carlson, adult enrichment supervisor with the Community Education Division of the Cottage Grove, Minnesota School System; and Kathy Thiel, with The Knowledge Network in Albany, New York.

Many with the various branches of the Learning

Annex have contributed. Jillian Greene, with the Learning Annex in Los Angeles, has been especially supportive. Strong support has also come from David Serstree, with the Learning Annex in Toronto.

Other continuing education center executives who have supported mystery shopping as a subject of study and Jim Poynter and this book in bringing mystery shopping to many include: Bob Walling and Carole Dorras, of Sage Ways in Albuquerque; Shelley Redmond and Barbara Stapf, with Open U in Minneapolis; Debra Leopold, of First Class, Inc. in Washington, D.C.; Derek Selbo and Paul Picone, formerly co-owners of The Knowledge Shop in Orlando; Bart Brodsky, with the Open Exchange in Berkeley; Lauren Young, with the Boston Center for Adult Education; Kay Morse, with Wichita (Kansas) Free University; and Catherine Cook, formerly with The Learning Exchange in Sacramento.

Special thanks go to my wife, Sorore, and my sons, Lewis, Robert, and Michael. It is probably never easy to live with an author who works from home. They are thanked for their continuing patience and understanding.

Foreword to the Fourth Edition

This was the first book written about how to become a mystery shopper that had an ISBN number (International Standard Book Number), was published by a major publisher, and has been available at bookstores throughout North America. It has been in such demand that the entire first printing sold out in less than two years, and both the second and third editions sold out even more rapidly.

One of the best measures of a book about how to get a job is the reaction of employers. So many mystery shopping company owners have been pleased with the work done for them by mystery shoppers who entered the field as a result of reading the first three editions of this book that they now recommend it to everyone who calls or writes asking how to get into mystery shopping. An author can't ask for a higher compliment.

The publishing of the book has taught us several things. Perhaps most important is that there is a great unmet demand. Mystery shopping companies need qualified shoppers to work for them, and individuals who want to do a good job as mystery shoppers are in abundance. However, the task of bringing the two together has not been easy.

There are many firms that sell lists of mystery shopping companies; sometimes these list sellers also include a few pages of information on how a person can become a mystery shopper. In most cases, however, the information is misleading, making it sound as if you don't have to do anything to collect huge amounts of money and keep extremely valuable merchandise. And the lists are of limited or no value. They sometimes include the names, addresses, and phone numbers of thousands of mystery shopping companies—many of which no longer even exist. They don't tell you that many of the companies listed only hire shoppers who live in a single town or village. Or that the companies that hire from a large geographical area frequently only hire experienced mystery shoppers. Almost without exception, the information on companies listed by these list sellers has never been cleared with anyone affiliated with the company before it was published and sold.

The end result has been a disservice to everyone except the sellers—who have sometimes made substantial amounts of money from the lists. The buyers of the lists (would-be mystery shoppers) usually do not get work, because the companies they apply with no longer exist, do not hire in their area, or only hire experienced shoppers.

Mystery shopping company owners have become frustrated. Staggering numbers of unqualified people with no knowledge about what mystery shoppers really need to do call and write them, expecting to receive large salaries and shopping money in the return mail. Some executives have gone so far as to change their addresses and phone numbers because they are inundated with unqualified applicants as a result of their corporate name and address being on so many lists.

And the biggest problem in the industry continues unabated. What is the biggest problem? Tom Jensen, the owner of a mystery shopping company in Ohio, put it correctly when he said, "I didn't know when I started this business that the hardest part of the job is finding qualified mystery shoppers."

This book is a strong effort at rectifying the problem. It provides a wealth of information about mystery shopping, what it takes to get the job, and how one can make real money from the job. In addition, it prepares readers to become the kinds of shoppers that mystery shopping companies like to hire. The companies listed are few—compared with those on the plethora of lists that are sold—but an executive with each firm has been contacted and has agreed on the wording that appears. Without exception, mystery shopping company executives have gone over the listings in detail and approved the information's accuracy. And all have indicated that they hire people who are *new* to mystery shopping. By following the advice in this book, those who are seeking mystery shopping jobs are getting them and company executives who are seeking qualified mystery shoppers are finding them.

But the book does more than list reputable, precleared companies and tell readers how to get a first job in the industry. In addition, it explains how to do that job and do it so well that you land job after job. It tells readers how to move up to better paying mystery shopping companies and how to maximize income from mystery shopping. It also includes valuable tips from readers who have been successful as mystery shoppers. Many are more successful and make more money than they ever expected. (See the sample letter received in early 1998 on page xvii.)

This is what a book on how to get a job in a field of interest should do. It should be so good that it has the power to change the lives of readers in a positive manner. And in that regard, the first three editions have done their job. Many readers have written saying that *Mystery Shopping* has been a positive influence and that they have succeeded in getting, keeping, and moving up in the mystery shopping jobs they wanted to get. What more can one ask?

The only answer to that question is simply the word: **MORE!** And the fourth edition does offer more—much more. There's more information on mystery shopping specialties and how to get shopping assignments in these specialty areas. And there's a new chapter on "tools of the trade." As mystery shopping matures as an industry, more items of equipment have become available that mystery shoppers can use to make the job easier. Computerization is beginning to become a way of life for an increasing number of mystery shopping companies. The fourth edition provides more than twice the number of electronic contacts for mystery shopping companies as compared to the third edition.

We have received letters from mystery shoppers indicating that they are increasingly using this book as a reference. Sure, most who buy it read it from cover to cover so that they can be knowledgeable and so that they can get started as mystery shoppers right away. But many of our readers also say that they use this book as a guide, referring to it again and again as they move into some of the more advanced areas of mystery shopping. For these people, the book has been brought out in a sturdy hardback edition for the first time with the fourth edition. We want you to be able to reference this book for many years to come.

As successful and beneficial as the first three editions were, it is hoped and expected that this fourth edition will top the first three. It is expected that an even greater percentage of those who buy this book will reach and exceed their add-on income goals. And it is expected that not only will the owners of mystery shopping companies continue to be happy with the work performed by the people who read this edition of the book, but that the owners of the add-on companies will also experience the same pleasure with the output of readers who work with them.

You can help. We are eager to hear your suggestions on additional information you'd like to see in the next edition or on information that needs further explanation. We want to hear your success stories and glean your useful mystery shopping tips. We try to produce a new, updated edition of *Mystery Shopping* every two years, and the chances are good that your suggestions will be included in the next edition. In this way, you will have contributed to those who come after you—a goal many who are professionals seek to attain.

Send your suggestions to: Jim Poynter, Post Office Box 40484, Denver, Colorado 80204. I thank you in advance for your suggestions.

Robert W. Fowler

January 19, 1998

Jim Poynter
PO Box 40484
Denver, CO 80204

Dear Jim,

I vividly recall a statement you made during your presentation at First Class in Washington, D.C. last fall—"you cannot make a full-time job out of this"! Well, if my current situation holds true, I will be very close to making this a part-time job with full-time pay.

Using your guidance, I wrote letters to all the companies listed in your book. I received replies from two companies within six weeks and now work regularly for one over 30 times a month. Most of these are quick and easy within a short drive of my home. Using that experience, I recently began working for a major real estate firm performing open house shops two Sundays each month. For this I receive $100 plus mileage for each day.

This week I will become an employee of a major retailer performing shops in their establishments. I will be paid an hourly wage plus mileage and work between 15 to 20 hours weekly. Again, I obtained this position by stating my experience on cover letters (the one thing during my interviews that impressed employers the most? My refusal to name the companies I work with).

I am now about to send follow-up letters to the companies listed in your book, stating my references and requesting assignments. I never really expected it to be this easy. With a couple more companies under my belt, I'm confident I can make this a rewarding occupation that I can work around my main focus in life, sculpturing.

I have enclosed a check for $19.95 for your newsletter. If it's anything like the book, I'm confident I can obtain many more assignments.

Sincerely,

Robert W. Fowler

Robert W. Fowler

Now go out there and do it. Become an excellent mystery shopper. And have fun at it. Yes, enjoy mystery shopping. It is probably, to coin a word made up by my youngest son, the "funnest" job you will ever have!

— Jim Poynter

CHAPTER 1

WHAT IS MYSTERY SHOPPING?

Not Just Fine Dining

I like to eat. Perhaps you do, too. Each month my wife and I are asked to visit at least one multistar restaurant—and we agree to do so. We are usually instructed to have our car parked by the restaurant's valet service. We do. The mystery shopping company assignment executive asks us to stop at the restaurant's bar for drinks and an appetizer before dinner—and we oblige. We are told to order salads, a multicourse meal, and wine with dinner—and, of course, we follow the instructions. The company exec advises that dessert and drinks should follow the meal. Not reluctantly, we agree.

When the meal is over, I pay the bill using my credit card (adding the tip, making sure it is included on the bill). A few hours later, I write a report detailing all aspects of the dining experience. I complete an expense report—including the cost of cash tips for the valet, perhaps the maitre d', the wine steward, and others whose tip would not normally be included on the bill. Copies of the mystery shopping dining report, the restaurant bill, the expense report, and the credit card receipt are made for my records. Originals are mailed to the mystery shopping company, and copies are placed in my home file.

Between five and six weeks later, I receive a check from the mystery shopping company. The check covers all expenses plus remuneration for writing the shopping report. The only problem my wife and I have found is determining who will be the designated driver.

If you like to eat, you will love mystery shopping. Paul, a single man in Houston, complains that his refrigerator is empty. He eats out at quality restaurants every night thanks to mystery shopping companies. He eats many lunches at both full-service and fast food restaurants as well. And recently, he noted, he has been asked to eat breakfasts, too. Paul writes a report after each of these meals and not only does he not have to fill his refrigerator, but he gets checks for eating these meals and writing about his eating experiences. Best of all, notes Paul, he can bring his dates to the kind of restaurants he never felt he could afford to patronize on a regular basis before.

The only problem, Paul confided in a recent conversation, is that he is getting bigger. But he thinks he has solved that problem as well. Recently, Paul accepted a series of assignments shopping health clubs. With each club visited, Paul goes through some form of exercise or visits an aerobic or other activity-oriented class.

So he eats lunch and then goes to a club; eats dinner and goes to a club. Paul says, "It works." But perhaps most importantly, he is finally keeping to a set weight (not gaining) and he is making money.

But mystery shopping is more than fine dining and health clubs. It is also an opportunity to buy from a wide variety of retailers—and keep the goods. Sheila works for a mystery shopping company that gives her a monthly budget. One month her budget was $120. She spends a specified amount in each of several departments in a mid-scale department store. If she wants to spend more than the allotted amount, she can do so, but the additional money will be at her own expense. Sometimes she is given total freedom as to what to buy; other times she is instructed to purchase specific items. For example, one month she was told to buy a pair of men's socks in the men's clothing department. Sheila, an older single woman, says that her relatives have always loved her, but now they love her even more. It is like Christmas every day. She can't wear men's socks—but her brother-in-law can. She doesn't play with children's toys, but her nieces and nephews do. Sheila's relatives get lots of presents. Meanwhile, Sheila gets lots of checks for writing reports about her mystery shopping experiences.

Mystery shoppers collect many new goods—often things they never expected to buy. And, they receive a large array of services—often services they would not otherwise have spent the money to purchase. For many of the things they regularly would spend money on, they now get reimbursed in full. Shoppers say that their cars have never been cleaned so often, lubed so frequently, or had the tires balanced so regularly. They

spend weekends vacationing in local hotels conducting hotel shops. Coworkers are impressed with their image because they receive so many opportunities to get their shirts starched, blouses dry cleaned, and other articles of apparel cleaned as a result of the many dry cleaning assignments they receive. And when it comes time to buy a new car, they know exactly which car they want to purchase because they have shopped for so many new cars. They become experts on wines, gourmet foods, and designer fashions. In essence, they become expert shoppers who are paid to shop.

In addition to services, mystery shoppers enjoy getting free items with almost every assignment they complete. But don't expect to redo your whole house with what you get as a mystery shopper. Most of the items you get to keep are inexpensive purchases. And it seems that mystery shopping companies are in cahoots with one another when it comes to what they ask you to buy. Before I started mystery shopping, my wife and I had a first aid kit in our home. Now, we have one in every room and in every car—and our relatives and friends are getting many more first aid kits from us than they really need. First aid kits, like socks, are inexpensive items and a surprising number of retailers carry them. The mystery shopping companies seem to be enamored with such items.

The Move Toward Providing a Shopping Budget

While the vast majority of mystery shopping companies will ask shoppers to buy one or more specific items when they undertake a shopping assignment, a few companies have started a move toward giving shoppers a budget. For example, instead of asking the shopper to purchase a pair of men's socks from the men's department of a department store, they instruct the shopper to purchase any item he or she wishes to buy from the men's department as long as the cost does not exceed $15. The budget is usually fairly low (typically between $15 and $25), but the shopper is not locked into buying a specific item. Although the mystery shopper may not find anything he or she wants in the department shopped (the single female with an assignment to purchase from the men's department, for example) or within the budget provided, most shoppers are much happier with receiving a budget and the freedom to buy anything in the department within that budget rather than being assigned to buy a specific item.

While there are only a few mystery shopping companies that are providing budgets rather than specific purchase item assignments, some of them have even improved on the budget concept. They allow mystery shoppers to buy anything the shopper wishes to purchase, even if the item is over the budget. However, the mystery shopper must pay the difference between the budgeted amount and the actual cost if the purchase is over budget. This arrangement allows shoppers to almost always find something they like and get it at a good price (the retail price less the mystery shopping assignment budget).

I frequently shop Sears Roebuck & Company. A few years ago, I received an assignment to buy something in the costume jewelry department. My budget was $20. Usually when I have an assignment to buy an item in the costume jewelry department, my wife places an order for something she'd like. However, this time I splurged on myself. I collect tie tacks, and I found one that I really liked for $31. I bought it. The mystery shopping company reimbursed me for $20 of the cost (my budget for that assignment), and I was able to get a nice tie tack by paying only the additional $11 out of pocket.

Almost all mystery shoppers prefer having a budget, being able to purchase over the budget, and paying the difference between the budget and the actual cost themselves. This gives mystery shoppers a maximum of opportunity to buy items that they really want. However, today only a few mystery shopping companies have adopted this *budget-plus* concept. For the sake of mystery shoppers, it can be hoped that more mystery shopping companies will move in this direction.

Honesty and Theft Prevention Shopping

But mystery shopping is more than reporting on service and the quality/price of food and merchandise. Mystery shoppers may also elect to specialize in theft or embezzlement reduction shops. If you ask for one of these assignments, here's the routine: You buy some small item (a candy bar or a newspaper, for example) in a convenience store, pretend that you are in a hurry, pay for it in cash, and leave rapidly. As you get to the door, you turn to see what the store clerk does with the money. If the money goes into the clerk's pocket or purse instead of the cash register, that is the information that will verify the store owner's suspicions. On the other hand, if the purchase is rung up correctly and the money is placed into the cash register box, you will have provided the owner with a verification that his employee is honest.

Not long ago the owner of a mystery shopping company got a phone call from the president of an investment firm that owned a large number of gas stations in his state. The president explained that he desperately needed a mystery shopper to save his firm from continuing to pay huge fines. It seems the state had been sending in young people to buy cigarettes at his company's gas stations all over the state. When identification was not asked for, the firm got a fine of more than $100 per incident. And no matter how much training and supervision effort the company lavished on its employees, each month the total amount of fines kept growing. The president wanted to send a mystery shopper who looked under age, but was really not under age, into all of his gas stations to buy cigarettes. The shopper was to get the name (from the employee name tag) and description of each clerk who did not ask for identification prior to the cigarette sale.

The mystery shopping company gave the assignment to a young lady who was a freshman at a local university. Each Saturday she drove from one gas station to another buying cigarettes and writing reports about whether or not she was asked for her identification prior to the purchase. The cigarette mystery shopper made money for writing the reports as well as from reselling the cigarettes (since she didn't smoke) to the smokers in her dorm. Everybody was happy. The state fines to the investment firm's gas stations dried up, so the president of the investment firm was elated. The mystery shopping company made money, so the mystery shopping company owner was happy. And perhaps happiest of all was the college-student mystery shopper, who made more money than she ever thought possible from a part-time job.

But honesty and theft prevention is not limited to convenience stores and gas stations. It applies to any situation in which there is potential loss to a company due to theft or a lack of honesty. Checking on how well security guards do their job is another area of honesty and theft prevention. Every Saturday many mystery shoppers get up early. They drive to their city's downtown area, park outside of an office building, and wait in their cars until they see a group of people getting ready to enter the building. Then the shopper mixes with the group as they go into the building. As everyone gets onto the elevator, they sometimes wave at or speak to the building security guard whose duty desk is usually near the bank of elevators. If so, the mystery shopper will also wave or utter a greeting. Everyone takes the elevator to his or her floor. The mystery shopper has been given a floor number, an office number, and the name of a person who works in that office. The mystery shopper gets off the elevator, goes to the office, and, because it is Saturday, finds the door to the office is locked. The shopper waits for four to six minutes and then leaves. Back at the car, the shopper writes a report indicating that the security guard did not try to stop him or her and that during the four to six minutes of waiting, the guard did not come up to the office to investigate whether or not the mystery shopper had a right to have access to the office.

Sometimes, the security guard stops the mystery shopper before the shopper can get onto the elevator. The guard will check a list of people who are approved for access to the building; of course, the mystery shopper's name won't be on the list. However, sometimes the shopper may still be able to get access by claiming to have a meeting with someone who works in the office. When this happens, the shopper goes to the office and waits the required four to six minutes before returning to the car and writing a report, which truthfully states that the guard made an initial effort to turn the shopper away, but eventually let the shopper go up to the office after providing the name of an office employee.

For this short assignment—entering an office building without authorization and writing a report about their Saturday morning experience with a security guard in the building—mystery shoppers are frequently paid between $18 and $30. That's not bad pay for being kicked out of office buildings. But it gets better. Many mystery shopping companies will group these assignments, asking shoppers to visit several downtown office buildings on Saturdays. Shoppers who take these types of assignments can make a substantial amount of money on a Saturday morning.

Specialty Shops

There are many kinds of specialty shopping assignments. A few of these are food and beverage shops, department store and specialty store shops, hotel shops, real estate shopping, new car shops, car lubrication shops, grocery store shops, bank shops, dry cleaning shops, distance shopping, and gasoline purchase shops. While there are many other types of specialty shops a mystery shopper might be asked to undertake, together these constitute the vast majority of all shopping assignments.

FOOD AND BEVERAGE SHOPS

There are more shopping assignments that involve eating and drinking than any other type of assignment. Some say as many as 34 percent of all mystery shopping involves eating out. These assignments range from fast food to fine dining and everything in between. In fact, the first assignment for most mystery shoppers is typically a fast food assignment. Usually you will be asked to buy a burger, fries, and a coke (or something similar). You will be asked to complete a two- or three-page report noting what you ordered, how fast you received the order, who took the order, who filled the order, how well prepared the food and beverage were, if the restaurant was clean, if the restroom was clean and well stocked, if the signs were easy to understand, as well as answering a number of other questions. For completing the assignment on time and sending in your completed report on time, you will be reimbursed for your food and beverage and you will probably be paid between $2 and $5 for writing the report.

Most mystery shoppers don't like fast food assignments. The food is often bland. The restaurants are usually busy and noisy. The service is nonexistent. And the pay is not enough to make it worth completing the assignment. However, the vast majority of mystery shopping companies start new mystery shoppers with fast food assignments. Even shoppers who have substantial experience with other mystery shopping companies are usually started with fast food assignments when they go to work for a company for which they have not worked in the past. Mystery shopping executives want to see how well a shopper does with an "entry-level" assignment before giving a mystery shopper an assignment with one of their better clients. An example may help to put this point across.

When Nordstrom announced that it was going to build a new store in my city, my wife strongly suggested that I become a mystery shopper shopping Nordstrom.

Most stores will not give out the name of the mystery shopping company that has the contract to provide mystery shopping for them. However, I have a friend who shops Nordstrom in Seattle. She gave me the name of the mystery shopping company for which she was working. I phoned the company and asked for application forms. These were completed and returned, and a short time later, I got a call from the person with the company who gives out shopping assignments. He asked if I would like an assignment, and I said, "Yes, Nordstrom." He chuckled and said it was his company's policy not to give new shoppers assignments with their best clients. I protested that I was an experienced mystery shopper, providing a listing of many major mystery shopping companies for which I had worked. He calmly responded that it was his company's policy not to give shoppers who were new to his company assignments with their best clients. He told me that once I had a substantial amount of experience with his company then I might be able to get an assignment to shop Nordstrom.

I gave up and agreed to work my way up to the assignment I really wanted—Nordstrom. I asked him what my first assignment would be. "Taco Bell," he responded. I accepted, and he told me which Taco Bell and what I was to purchase. A few days later, I received a package in the mail from his mystery shopping company. This is normal. Most companies will send mystery shoppers a shopping report to fill out, a confirmation sheet detailing where and when the shopping assignment is to be completed, and what should be purchased. But this package was the largest one I had ever received from a mystery shopping company. I opened it up, looked inside, and found a thermometer. They wanted me to take the temperature of the burrito to make sure it was hot enough. I wondered how I could do that and not be identified as the mystery shopper. While I was pondering, I explored the package further. I pulled out something else. It was a scale. They wanted me to weigh the burrito to make sure it had enough ingredients. I had never before (or since) received a thermometer and scale in a package from a mystery shopping company. However, I decided to go to the drive-in, order the burrito, park my car, and then take the burrito's temperature and weight. After that, I went into the Taco Bell and checked out the condition of the restroom, the cleanliness of the dining room, the speed at which people were served, and all the other things mystery shoppers are asked to do. It took a lot of time, but I completed the assignment and was paid $4 for my report. And I got the cost of the burrito and a soft drink reimbursed.

After Taco Bell, I progressed to cafeteria service type restaurants. Next came inexpensive specialty shops. Then I moved up to restaurants where there were servers and a sit-down menu. Mid-level chain department stores were the next step up the ladder, followed by bank shopping assignments. Finally, I got to fine dining and Nordstrom shopping assignments. This type of progress up the mystery shopping ladder is typical. Usually there will be a mixture between food and beverage establishments and other types of assignments. Many mystery shopping companies will give you an assortment of assignments as you progress, but will concentrate on those types of assignments you seem to do best.

Gourmet restaurant shopping assignments are my favorite types of assignments. The report form is usually five or six pages long, and the pay ranges from $20 to $45 for writing the mystery shopping report. You will be asked to call ahead to make a reservation. A full page (sometimes as much as two pages) of questions will be asked about your call for a reservation. Fortunately, you can be looking at the questionnaire while you are on the phone.

When you arrive, it will be expected that you have your car parked by the valet and that you tip the valet in cash. The amount of your tip (usually both in and out of the restaurant) should be added to

your bill submitted to the mystery shopping company.

When you arrive, you will want to note the time and the name of the person who greets you. In fact, you will be expected to remember the names of all employees who serve you in some way. Most fine dining assignments have no limit on what you can spend, and you are expected to order expensive before-meal drinks, appetizers, entrees, desserts, and after-meal drinks. It is better to not go overboard. Although the instructions will usually say that you may order anything you wish to order, it is better to order one of the less expensive bottles of wine (even though the wine list will usually carry wines that cost in excess of $250 per bottle).

There will usually be two or three pages of questions relating to what happened when you ordered your before-meal drinks and appetizer, another couple of pages relating to your main course and side dishes, and several pages of questions related to your dessert and after-meal drinks. There will be questions relating to the image of the restaurant, the degree to which a manager was seen to be in charge, and questions regarding the cleanliness of the restrooms. Review the questions on your shopping report form *before* you arrive at the restaurant and try to remember the details so that you can accurately report what happened. Many mystery shoppers wear a tape recorder while undertaking fine dining shopping assignments and are able to get the details on tape unobtrusively. This technique will be discussed later in the book.

A shopper is usually paid between $20 and $45 to write a report on a gourmet restaurant experience, and it will normally take between forty-five minutes and an hour to write a good report. Most mystery shoppers maintain that the compensation for writing the report does not justify the time, energy, and effort required to write the report. However, unless a good report is written, one should not expect to receive another fine dining assignment. And the excellent food, wine, alcoholic drinks, and ambiance are well worth it. If you were paying for the fine dining experience yourself (not being reimbursed by the mystery shopping company), you would have to budget between $125 and $300 for you and your spouse or friend. A fine dining experience is one well deserving the work to get the assignment and the work required in writing a good mystery shopping report.

DEPARTMENT STORE AND SPECIALTY SHOPS

In the beginning, mystery shoppers will get assignments for shopping in the less expensive specialty shops and chain department stores. They will usually be asked to purchase small, inexpensive items, such as socks, handkerchiefs, scarves, picture frames, and so forth. Although you may shop in a chain store each month, you will rarely shop in the same department of the same store more than once every nine or ten months. For example, there are five Sears Roebuck stores in the metropolitan area in which I live. Two of them are so far away I won't shop in them. However, I shop in at least one and often in two of the other three stores every month. If I am asked to buy something in the small appliances department from the store that is nearest to me this month, I will not buy anything from that store's small appliance department again for nearly a year. However, next month I may get an assignment in the same store to purchase something in the costume jewelry department. Or I may not get any assignment in that store until the month after next. Executives of mystery shopping companies do not want sales clerks to see the same shopper too often. If so, they might perceive that that shopper is a mystery shopper.

As you build your experience in doing a good job shopping in the less expensive specialty stores and department stores, you should be able to move up to the more expensive specialty stores and department stores.

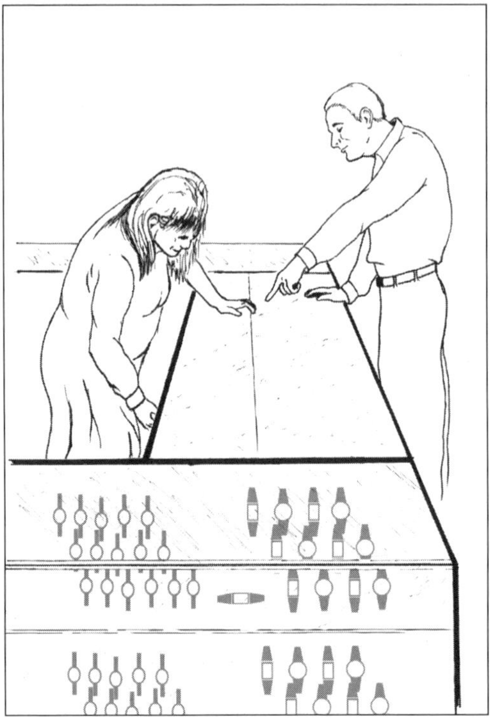

Eventually, you can expect to be shopping in the top name stores in your city. Of course, you may still elect to shop in the less expensive stores you like to shop in if you wish. Although most of my specialty and department store shopping (after more than nine years as a mystery shopper) is with the better stores, I still shop at Sears and a number of other similar stores.

One of the best things about shopping specialty stores and department stores is that you will eventually be able to group assignments. These days when I go to a big shopping center, I will usually carry out mystery shopping assignments with two or three specialty stores and an equal number of department stores. Our downtown has a walking mall that is cut off from automobile traffic. On a recent visit to that mall, I completed eight assignments. In the next chapter, the technique of grouping assignments to maximize income for the time spent shopping will be discussed in detail. Taking a large number of specialty store and department store shopping assignments is one of the best ways of grouping assignments.

HOTEL SHOPS

My wife saves our burned out light bulbs. It isn't because she has weird savings habits. It is because I do hotel shops. I am one of the few people I know (the others are also mystery shoppers) who travel to cities throughout North America carrying two burned out light bulbs in my suitcase. I sometimes wonder what the customs agent will say if my luggage is opened when going to Canada or back to the United States and the agent discovers one or both of my burned out light bulbs. Will the customs agent really believe, I wonder, that they are a required part of my mystery shopping equipment? And that bag of lint I carry from the clothes washer/dryer. That is also essential equipment. (Just in case the agent doesn't believe my explanations for these unusual travel items, I pack a copy of this book with a paper clip on this page.)

Hotel shops can be fun. Typically, it is the better quality hotel chains that contract for hotel shops. The mystery shopper is expected to act like a typical, but finicky, hotel guest. Ideally, the shopper will be a person who might normally stay at the hotel anyway. Usually the shopper is expected to check in for a two-night stay. A few days before check-in, you are expected to call the reservations office and reserve a standard room (usually nonsmoking). Two or more pages of the report will be dedicated to asking about the call to make a reservation. Another part of the report will ask you to evaluate the check-in experience. The shopper is expected to ask for a number of special requests—for example, a wake-up call (even if there is an alarm clock in the room), a quiet room, an iron, laundry that must be returned the same day, and so forth.

Once inside the room, the shopper goes to work. One or more room service meals will be ordered. The shopper may complain that he or she cannot operate the television set, control the room temperature, or get the shower water to the right degree. Burned out light bulbs (from the inventory in my suitcase) will be substituted for good bulbs. Calls to the front desk, engineering, the concierge, and the bell station will request help, service, or information. Tiny items placed strategically on the floor and in other locations will tell the shopper whether or not the room has been cleaned and vacuumed thoroughly (this is where the bag of lint comes in handy). Typically, the shopper will be asked to eat in several of the hotel's restaurants, to patronize the hotel health club, and to buy something in the hotel gift shop. I especially like it when they insist that I get a massage. Although hotel shops ask the mystery shopper to report on a wide variety of hotel facilities and services, they are among the best paying of all shopping assignments.

REAL ESTATE SHOPPING

Real estate shops come in two basic forms: new home shopping assignments and shopping for an apartment. Mystery shopping assignments calling for one or more

apartment shops are usually short in duration and pay substantially less than new home shopping assignments. Most of the time, the key factor being judged is how well the apartment agent did her job in showing apartments in the building or complex. Many apartment leasing companies have a specific set of procedures that they want followed. There are ethical, equal opportunity, and legal-oriented issues and questions that need to be considered, as well. Because mystery shopping companies that specialize in apartment rental shopping frequently have a large number of customers (apartment complexes) in metropolitan areas, mystery shoppers who specialize in apartment shopping can sometimes group assignments and complete four or five apartment shops on a Saturday or a Sunday. When this is the case, weekend shoppers sometimes find that they can earn as much in one day of apartment mystery shopping as they earn in two days during the week working at their full-time job.

The second type of real estate shop is far more involved, pays far better per shopping assignment, but can rarely be grouped with other shopping assignments for multiassignment pay. This is new home shops, and the client is usually a new homebuilder. Typically a builder/developer will contract to have a shopper (and the shopper's spouse) visit three new homes. A different builder will build each home, but each home will be of the same type (ranch, bi-level, or tri-level, for example). Each home will be new, and each home will be in both the same part of the city and priced at about the same cost. The shopper will be asked to report on what features he or she liked best (and least), how appealing the financing package was, how well the agent showed the property, and a wide range of other questions. Mystery shopping companies will relay the reports to the real estate clients who, by reading the reports, will understand what their competitors are building and charging, how their staff members are showing their homes, and how they compare with their competitors in the eyes of mystery shoppers. Real estate client company executives will then have a better idea of what types of houses, townhouses, and condominiums to build, what features to include, and how to price their condos, townhouses, and homes so that they will sell fast and sell profitably.

This is almost the only type of shopping assignment where the mystery shopper is expected to bring a note pad and take notes. You will need the notes. There will normally be many pages of questions asked about each new home visited. The complexity of the report, the time it takes to complete the shopping assignment (and the report), and the high pay earned by shoppers is about the same for hotel shops and for new home shopping assignments. Usually only experienced shoppers are used for these types of specialized shopping assignments, but most shoppers who do hotel and new home shops find that the income per assignment is more than worth the work.

NEW CAR SHOPS

New car shops can be educational. For those who are planning on buying a new car in the near future, you can get a good idea as to the benefits of a wide range of cars if you take on a multitude of new car shopping assignments. In addition, I am convinced that completing regular new car shops makes you far less vulnerable to the high-pressure sales techniques some salespeople use. The approach is exactly like it would be if you really were buying a new car. You look at several models and allow yourself to be guided by the salesperson. Your report will ask if the salesperson suggested several models, showed you the specific model you were instructed to express interest in, discussed features of the models, and made an effort to get you to buy at the time you were in the dealership. You are expected to take the car on a test drive (usually of city streets and highway) and to bring the sales transaction clear up to the point where you will be asked to sign on the dotted line. Then, you back away, giving an

appropriate excuse. New car shops take longer than most shopping assignments. The pay ranges from about $45 up to more than $150.

CAR LUBRICATION SHOPS

It has been a number of years since I paid for (and was not reimbursed for) one of my cars to be lubricated. Almost every month I get a car lubrication assignment from some mystery shopping company. Before I was a mystery shopper, I had all my cars lubricated (one for my wife, one for me, and one for each child between the ages of sixteen and twenty-two). It was not inexpensive. Now, I get reimbursed for each car lubrication, and I am paid to write a report about the lube job. Yes, I go to places that are not quite as convenient as the place where I regularly took my cars before be-

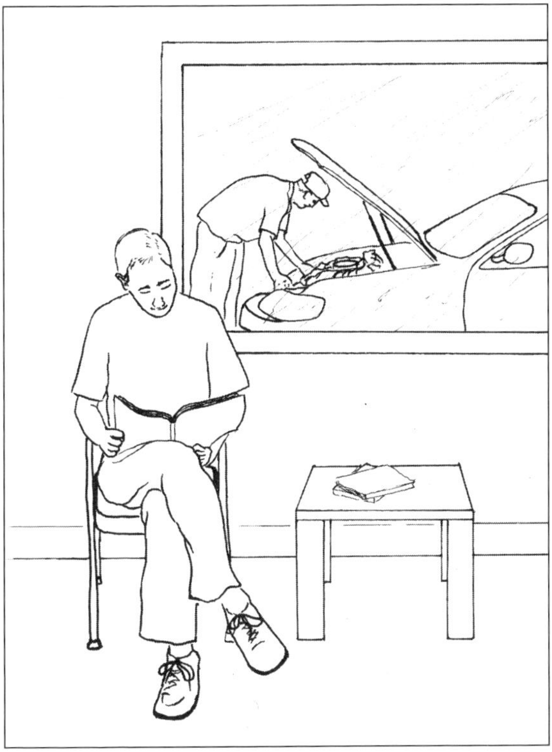

coming a mystery shopper. But the lube places I go to are never more than a mile out of the way between my office and my home. As with so many other products and services I would buy even if I were not a mystery shopper, the savings from having mystery shopping companies pay for these expenses really add up.

GROCERY STORE SHOPS

Grocery store shopping assignments vary depending upon what the client is most interested in. One upscale, gourmet chain is concerned about selling items for which the validity date has expired. For that grocery store chain, the mystery shopping company tells

shoppers that they may buy up to $20 worth of groceries, but at least one item should be something with an expired validity date. Stocking clerks are expected to take items off the shelf if the validity date has expired, and checkout clerks are expected to catch items with an expired validity date when shoppers go through the checkout stands. However, the real key to getting items with expired validity off the shelves is to offer mystery shoppers $20 of free groceries when they find and purchase such items. The shopper is expected to fill out a questionnaire and to attach to the completed questionnaire the original expiration date seal.

Another major chain has a more wide-ranging list of concerns. Shoppers normally shop no more than once every three months, but mystery shoppers have a $35 budget and they are reimbursed for up to $35 of grocery expenses. Here the questionnaire asks whether or not shelves were fully stocked (if not, which ones needed stocking), if employees greeted customers in the store, if employees who were asked for directions to where food items were stocked actually went with the customer to show her where the items were stocked, and so forth. Although mystery shoppers are typically paid a small amount of money (usually up to $10) for writing the shopping report, for most people, the real remuneration is the groceries themselves.

BANK SHOPS

Most bank shopping assignments are straightforward. Shoppers are instructed to open a new account, then they fill out a shopping report form, which includes a number of questions regarding how they were handled by bank employees whose job it is to assist in opening an account. Occasionally, other banking tasks are assigned to mystery shoppers. For example, they may pretend to be shopping for a home loan or they may ask for assistance in transferring monies abroad. Of course, they won't actually transfer monies to another country or apply for a loan; they simply ask for information and report on how their request was handled.

Most bank mystery shopping assignments pay from $20 to $30. A man in Los Angeles who took my mystery shopping course in the spring of 2001 said he was paid $1,000 for each of two bank shopping assignments he did in the L.A. area for the World Bank. He wanted to know how he could get other well-paying ($1,000 or more per assignment) mystery shopping

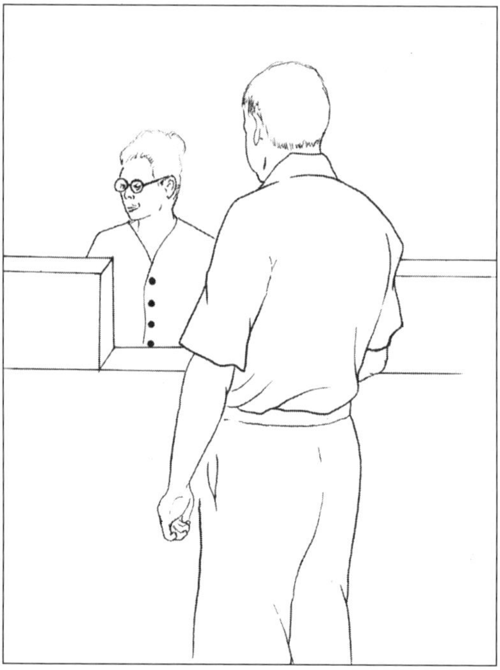

jobs. I had to tell him I also would like to know how to get $1,000 per assignment World Bank mystery shopping assignments. In all reality, I think the World Bank payment he reported receiving was either a fluke, or he did not correctly remember the amount of his payment. It would be better to count on getting from $20 to $30 and hope that some day the World Bank will brighten your day considerably.

DRY CLEANING SHOPS

If you reside in a major city, you know that dry cleaning is expensive. I pay for most items by check or credit card so that at the end of the year I can budget for the next year based on my expenditures during the previous year. Before becoming a mystery shopper, I was careful in my dry cleaning expenditures, often driving out of the way to patronize a less expensive dry cleaner. For the last several years, however, I have not concerned myself with the expense of dry cleaning. At least twice a month—sometimes three times a month—I get a dry cleaning assignment.

Normally I get a budget of $20 per shopping assignment, and I must include both dry cleaning and laundry. There are two reports. One covers the visit when clothing is dropped off, and the other covers the visit when clothing is picked up and paid for. I am asked time questions: When did you arrive? How long did you have to wait to be helped? What time did you leave the dry cleaners? I am also asked service questions: Did the person helping you wear a name tag? What was his or her name? Describe the person. Did they offer our special promotion? Did they tell you when your clothing could be picked up? Did they call you by name? And I am usually asked about the quality of the dry cleaning work.

After you do a dry cleaning assignment once, you will find future dry cleaning reports easy to complete. In addition to getting fully reimbursed (up to $20) for having my dry cleaning/laundry done, I am also paid to write a report about my dry cleaning/laundry experience. The payment usually ranges from $18 to $20.

DISTANCE SHOPPING

An increasing number of mystery shopping companies are moving into what is often called distance shopping. This is shopping by phone in most cases, but there are a few assignments calling for shopping by computer. In distance shopping, clients are evaluating

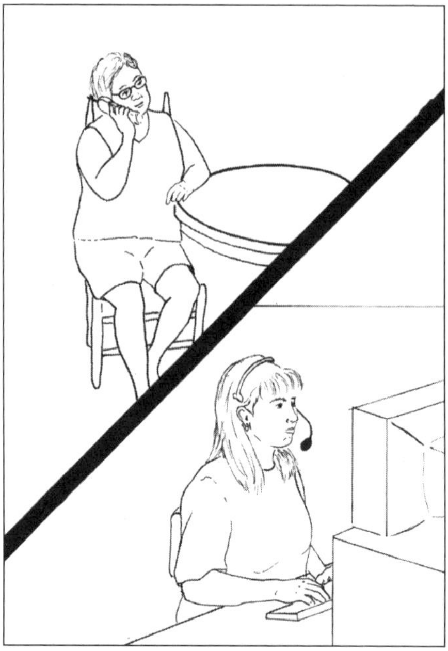

service. It is said that a smile can be sensed over the phone, and certainly the attitude of the person taking a telephone order is important. You will be asked how many rings it took before the phone was answered, whether or not you were put on hold, if you were transferred to one or more people, if the order taker was knowledgeable and could answer your questions. You will also be asked how long it took for you to receive the item ordered and what condition it was in when it arrived. Recently, some distance shopping is being done by computer, and mystery shoppers are beginning to get assignments to place computer-generated orders. It is similar in many ways to completing telephone orders. You either enter into a question/answer session online or via e-mail messages. Eventually, you order an item and report on delivery time and the condition of the product when it arrived.

While there are few mystery shopping companies that offer mystery shopping assignments by distance shopping, it is probable that the number of these shopping opportunities will increase with time. We are not far from the time when many people will have cameras attached to their home computers, and distance shopping will allow one to see both the salesperson and the item being purchased on the home computer screen. Internet sales are increasing every year, and it can be expected that it will be a major source of purchasing in the not-too-distant future.

GASOLINE PURCHASE SHOPS

Most shoppers like the idea of getting free gasoline, and with mystery shopping, free gas is now available. A few chain gasoline stations have contracted with mystery shopping companies to have mystery shoppers shop their stations. Typically, the shopper buys ten gallons of gas, pays for it, gets a receipt, fills out a shopping report, attaches the gasoline receipt to the report, and gets reimbursed for the ten gallons of gas. Plus the shopper is paid a nominal sum to fill out a short report on his gasoline buying experience. Shoppers can sometimes get several of these assignments a month making it hypothetically possible to not have to make any gasoline purchase that is not fully reimbursed.

Competitive Shopping

New home shopping assignments are quite frequently competitive shopping assignments. So are many department store and specialty shop mystery shopping assignments. In fact, competitive shopping is a form of mystery shopping that is growing in popularity with many shopping company clients. Everyone, it seems, wants to know as much as possible about their competitors—and mystery shopping is one of the best ways of finding out. Companies are anxious to know what their competitors are charging for the same (or similar) items. Mystery shoppers are asked to price items. Sometimes they will be asked to price the same or an equivalent item in as many as ten local stores. More often, however, they will be asked to compare the service and prices for several (usually not more than four) different products in up to three competing stores. Sometimes focus group training sessions follow competitive shopping—and the mystery shopper gets paid to do both. In a focus group training session, three or four mystery shoppers will meet with the executives of a retail store and will discuss what the shoppers found to be good and bad about their shopping experience—compared to shopping the store's competitors.

Mystery Shopping Is Growing in Popularity Because It Works

Both the concept of mystery shopping and the areas of mystery shopping specialization are growing in popularity. All predictions are that mystery shopping is the wave of the future because it is effective. Very simply, it works.

To understand why mystery shopping works, consider the case of a restaurant owner who purchased a failing restaurant in a major Midwestern city. Immediately after the purchase, he signed a contract with the largest mystery shopping company in the region. The two-year contract called for six mystery shops a week with each shopping assignment week running from Friday morning through Thursday evening. Since the restaurant is open seven days a week for lunches and dinners only, the owner specified he wanted the restaurant to be shopped for one meal a day (either lunch or dinner) for six of the seven days of the week. Each Monday morning the restaurant owner pays his entire staff to attend a staff meeting at 9 a.m. The focus of the meeting centers around the six reports received from mystery shoppers over the past week. The meeting starts with a recognition of and a "thank you" for the restaurant's "Star" employees for the week. Each shopper is asked to identify a "Star" employee—someone who shined during the shopping visit of the mystery shopper. At the Monday morning meeting the restaurant owner asks each of these "Star" employees to stand up. He congratulates and thanks each of the "Star" employees, and he hands each one a small cash reward. He then reads the comments of the mystery shoppers explaining why the particular person was considered an exceptional or "Star" employee.

The shopping report also asks mystery shoppers to identify the employee who provided the worst service during their visit and to explain what the problems were. The restaurant owner does not ask these people to stand up at the meeting. In fact, he does not even read out their names. Instead, sometime during the week, he will talk with each of these employees privately and discuss what the problems were and how changes might result in improvements. If several mystery shoppers name an employee as "worst employee" over a number of weeks, his or her employment may eventually be terminated.

At the staff meeting, the restaurant owner also highlights areas in which mystery shoppers indicate the restaurant either might need improvement or areas where improvement has been attained. For example, at one meeting he stated, "It looks like our portion control problem has been solved. The shoppers are reporting that their food portions were either sufficient or overly large, and none reported insufficient portions this past week. In looking at our food costs for the week, it appears you have been able to solve the portion control issue without creating overly expensive food costs. Congratulations and thanks." Whenever the owner brings up an area of concern, he either congratulates and thanks his employees for doing a good job or, if improvements are needed, he throws it back to the employees, saying, "What should we do about it?" The owner and employees discuss everything from the condition of the restrooms to food quality/quantity to service and valet parking.

CHAPTER 2

FINANCIAL AND RELATED MATTERS

How Much Money Can You Make?

UNREALISTIC AND REALISTIC AVERAGES

"*Earn $100,000 a year as a Mystery Shopper!*" screamed the headlines of the advertisement. Yes, rip-off companies, such as the one in New Orleans that placed this advertisement in women's magazines throughout North America, promise huge incomes from mystery shopping. Unfortunately, such promised incomes are way off from reality. The owner of a shopping company located near the headquarters of the New Orleans rip-off company once stated, "If I could make $100,000 a year as a mystery shopper, I would sell my mystery shopping company and work as a shopper for someone else." But, of course, he knows that mystery shoppers do not make such an elevated income.

So what *is* a realistic income from mystery shopping? The reality is that mystery shopping can provide a good add-on or second income, but mystery shoppers do not get rich. The average mystery shopper rarely brings in more than $500 or $600 per month. However, $100, $200, $400, or especially $600 added to one's current income can provide a nice lifestyle bonus.

Although not average, some shoppers have found that they can earn more from their part-time job of mystery shopping than they earn from their full-time job. On January 19, 1998, Robert Fowler of Greenbelt, Maryland, wrote, "I vividly recall a statement you made during your presentation at First Class in Washington, D. C. last fall (September 1997)—'You cannot make a full-time job out of this.' Well, if my current situation holds true, I will be close to making this a part-time job with full-time pay." He reached this income level in less than five months. At his request, I met with Bob before my next class in Washington, D. C., in September 1998. I was impressed with the amount of mystery shopping he was doing. He had quit his full-time job. But he also was working at mystery shopping substantially more than twenty hours a week. Bob consistently earns in the $3,000 a month range. However, most shoppers simply don't want to work as mystery shoppers as hard or as much as Bob does.

Soon after she took a class with me, Ann Gresham of Philadelphia started writing and calling to tell me about her multitude of successes in mystery shopping. She uses long lunch hours to undertake mystery shopping assignments. Every evening and almost all day every weekend she can be found completing mystery shopping assignments. She has told me on several occasions that she brings in between $3,000 and $3,200 a month as a mystery shopper—and I believe her. However, between her full-time job and her part-time job, Ann doesn't have much of a life other than work.

For every Robert Fowler or Ann Gresham who earn as much or more from part-time mystery shopping as they do from their full-time jobs, there are many more mystery shoppers who earn substantially less from their part-time mystery shopping job than from their full-time job. For the vast majority of shoppers, mystery shopping is simply a nice way to garner a comfortable additional income while enjoying the other many benefits of mystery shopping.

THE FINANCIAL VALUE OF ADD-ON BENEFITS

In addition to the money—getting paid to shop—mystery shoppers receive meals, services, and products free. When one adds the value of these, the real benefits of mystery shopping can be much more than the vast majority of other part-time jobs. The value can add up to $500 or $600 a month for many shoppers.

In addition, there are other, nonmonetary benefits. Do you hate your boss? How about a job where one almost never sees the boss? Would you like to choose your job assignments? You can. Experienced mystery shoppers frequently pick and choose their assignments based on phone conversations. Some experienced shoppers turn down many more assignments than they accept. In fact, this is one of the few jobs where you not only don't see the boss, but you can say "no" to the boss and still keep getting top paying assignments. Would you like to have fun on the job? Most experienced shoppers agree that mystery shopping is a lot of fun.

Would you like to schedule a substantial amount of

time off whenever *you* decide you want to take the time off? You can. Mary Ellis, a woman who started mystery shopping in her sixties after her last child had gone off to college, does just that. She said she had never worked outside the home, and her husband has always made a good income. But when the kids grew up and left home, she wanted to have something to do. Shopping had always been a pleasurable past time for Mary. So she became a mystery shopper—and a good shopper at that. "But the holidays are when my kids come back home to visit. That is *my* time," she stressed. "I want to be with my children and grandchildren. I call all the mystery shopping companies I work for and tell them not to give me any assignments between the tenth of December and the fourth of January. Come January 5th, the kids have gone back home and I am ready to shop again."

What other job gives you the option of calling in and saying you won't work for a period of several weeks of your choosing every year? In fact, when you think about it, what other occupation allows you to say, "no" to the boss, turn down work assignments you don't want to do, never see the boss, and still have lots of fun earning money? When the money and benefits are considered as a total package, it becomes obvious that mystery shopping is a wonderful way of life. One would be hard pressed to find a more delightful way to "moonlight."

THE PAY FOR INDIVIDUAL SHOPPING ASSIGNMENTS

Individual shopping assignments pay from very little to quite well. There are a few that allow you to keep the product or service, but pay nothing. However, these assignments are rare—fortunately. Some assignments pay as much as $30 for work that takes no more than ten minutes. That is a pay of $3 per minute (on an hourly basis it equates to $180 per hour). However, these assignments are also rare—unfortunately.

There are several levels of assignments. Generally speaking, new shoppers will receive assignments that pay little. Many of these will pay as little as $2 to $8, but some will pay as much as $19. Shoppers who have completed between five and ten assignments for a company may move into the beginning experienced category and will find a growing number of better-paying assignments available to them; the assignments that they receive will pay between $20 and $40 per assignment. It is generally the most experienced shoppers who get assignments paying more than $40 per assignment. A few assignments will pay more than $100 per assignment, but these lucrative assignments generally go to those shoppers who have completed forty to fifty assignments for a mystery shopping company.

Please remember that it rarely matters how many companies you have worked for. Each mystery shopping company will give you assignments (and pay) based on how many assignments you have completed with their company and how well you have completed the assignments. Fortunately, there are exceptions, and some shoppers have been able to move up rapidly. Most of these exceptions apply because you live in an area where the mystery shopping company has few or no other shoppers working with it. However, some mystery shopping companies will rapidly move shoppers up to better-paying assignments as soon as they determine a shopper is doing an exceptionally good job.

A GOOD POLICY

As noted earlier, there are some assignments that pay nothing. The only compensation is being able to keep the product or enjoy the service. In fact, there are mystery shopping companies that pay nothing to the shoppers who work for them. Every assignment from such a company is done with no compensation for writing mystery shopping reports. It is generally a good idea to avoid such assignments and such companies. The vast majority of mystery shopping companies pay a reasonable amount of money for writing mystery shopping reports.

One man once told me that he felt taking an assignment for which he would not be paid would be a good way to break into the field—that is, to get his first mystery shopping assignment. The probability is that he would get a first assignment right away. However, keep in mind that many mystery shopping companies find their most difficult job is finding good mystery shoppers. Most companies are always looking for more shoppers so that they can discover the "gems"—those shoppers who do an excellent job. Therefore, most people who have no experience get experience right away without having to resort to working for a company that does not pay shoppers to write reports. The real problem is that if you work for no pay for your first assignment, you may be tempted to accept a no-pay assignment a second time and you could find yourself working for no pay on a continuing basis. Therefore, it is a good policy to avoid working for no pay altogether and especially for a first assignment.

There is an exception, however. When the product or service you receive is quite valuable, you might want to accept a no-pay assignment just to get the item or service. For example, I lecture throughout North America. In most cases, I pay for my own lodging. The average cost is approximately $90 per night. I am frequently in a city for two nights. In many cases, I shop hotels in the city where I am lecturing. In most cases the compensation—the pay for writing a report about my hotel stay—is generous. It should be. The reports tend to be long. However, there are times when I am unable to get a paying assignment to conduct a hotel shopping assignment in one or more of the cities where I go. In such cases, I will sometimes accept a hotel shopping assignment with a company that does not pay. The hotel shopping reports for that company are short (a half page) and easy to complete (most are "yes" or "no" questions). When accepting this no-pay hotel shopping assignment, I find that I have saved approximately $180 in hotel costs for completing an assignment that takes little time and effort. In other words, it is a good policy to avoid no-pay assignments, but after you are an experienced shopper, it won't hurt to evaluate no-pay assignment offers and determine whether or not the product or service is valuable enough to you to undertake the assignment anyway.

HOW THE SYSTEM WORKS

It is good to know how the system works. I am often asked to speak about mystery shopping at meetings of business people. In 1999, at a quality control conference for CEOs of small businesses held at a university in Utah, an attendee asked: "I know I need to adopt a mystery shopping program for my company. When I contacted mystery shopping companies, the prices quoted were all over the place. A friend of mine owns a local fast food franchise. I knew it was mystery shopped. So I talked with my friend about it. The price he told me he pays per mystery shop was much less than any of the quotes I received. How can I get the kind of price he receives, and how do I know that what I get will really give me the kind of feedback that will make the mystery shopping program worthwhile?"

These are good questions, and they are the kinds of questions business people face when considering the adoption of a mystery shopping program. I told him that the chains of fast food companies have substantial pricing clout. They have literally thousands of fast food franchises throughout North America and in many other countries. Typically, they contract to have several shopping assignments for each franchisee each month. With these numbers, they can negotiate with many mystery shopping companies and get extremely low costs per shop for their franchisees. They require each franchisee to participate in the mystery shopping program, but they know that many of the franchisees will ignore the mystery shopping reports they receive. Many franchise owners are absentee or not working owners. They may visit the fast food place that they own only once or twice a year. For some, all they care about is that the franchise is making money. Therefore, having a top quality program is not the most important concern when many fast food franchisers contract for a nationwide mystery shopping program.

Cost is important. It is for that reason that most new mystery shoppers find themselves with a first assignment to shop a fast food place, and the shopper is paid as little as $2 to complete the assignment.

The businessman asking the series of questions does not have the number of franchises to get a per shopping assignment price quote anywhere near the inexpensive rate given to a major chain of fast food restaurants. But in this business, the client gets what he pays for. The businessman wanted a mystery shopping program that would "give (him) the kind of feedback that (would) make the mystery shopping program worthwhile." We, the shoppers, may tell ourselves that we will always strive to do a good job no matter what we are paid. That is nice theory. However, in reality, mystery shoppers, like other employees, tend to do a better job when they are paid well. For a business to have a mystery shopping program that is effective (worthwhile), shoppers need to do a good job. And, the more we are paid, the better the job we do. Therefore, I told the businessman to not take the least expensive quote he received. Instead, I said, look seriously at the five most expensive companies. Talk with the executives and tell them exactly what kind of feedback you want. Ask for their ideas. Concentrate on how you can get feedback that will allow you to make the changes that will produce more repeat client purchases for you. After all, that is the kind of result a quality control program should deliver. Set up a method of measuring repeat client purchases both before and after starting the mystery shopping program. Within two to three months, you should know if the mystery shopping program is paying off for you. But I told him that if he buys on price alone, I could guarantee his mystery shopping program would fail.

THE DOLLAR PER MINUTE RULE

As a shopper, if money is important (for some it is more so than for others), the dollar per minute rule is suggested. This means that one averages the income from mystery shopping assignments and works toward a goal of getting paid an average of one dollar for each minute worked. In other words, it forces mystery shopping to pay approximately $60 per hour. The dollar a minute rule requires the shopper to track the amount of time spent shopping and filling out shopping reports. Normally, drive time to and from the assignment is not included, just as it is rarely included by employers who pay their staff members a monthly salary. Nevertheless, one must always be aware that driving to and from mystery shopping assignments can consume many hours each month, and one can expect to receive no pay for the time one is on the road driving.

When you receive a call with an assignment, mentally calculate the approximate time it will take to complete the shop and the report. Then divide the pay by the estimated number of work minutes. For example, if you calculate that the shopping time will be twenty minutes and the report will take fifteen minutes to complete, you will have a total time of thirty-five minutes. If the pay for this assignment is $35, your income will be $1 per minute. If the pay is $17 or $18 for the assignment, your income will be approximately fifty cents per minute. And if your pay is more than $35, your income will be in excess of one dollar per minute.

When you first start working as a mystery shopper,

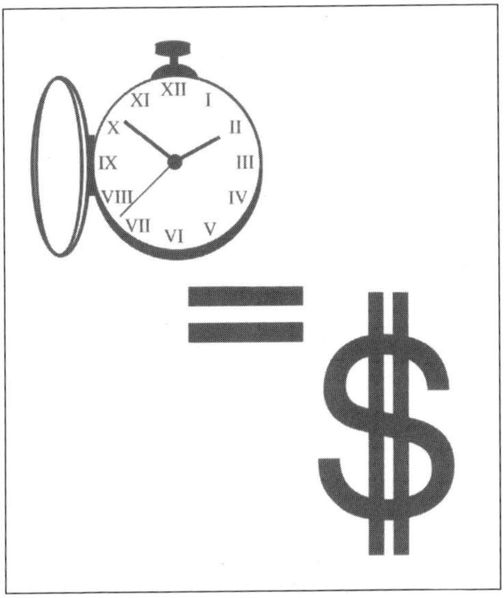

it may be difficult to estimate what your income per minute will be. As you gain experience, however, you will be surprised at how close you can get to estimating your per minute income. In the beginning, you will probably want to accept any and all assignments just so that you can get your foot in the door with mystery shopping companies. This is almost always a good idea. Once you know a company, you will know which of its assignments pay well per minute and which ones don't. You will then be in a position to turn down the low paying jobs and accept those that pay well.

There are some companies, however, that pay poorly for all of their assignments. It may take a few months to learn how to recognize them, but soon you will be able to weed out the low-paying companies rapidly—sometimes from the first time they call you.

There are exceptions to the dollar a minute rule that you might want to consider. When you start with a company, you will start at the bottom with the lowest paying assignments. You may not want to get paid $2 for a fast food assignment, but unless you take such an assignment, it is unlikely that you will ultimately get better-paying assignments. I adopt the policy of exempting from my dollar a minute calculations those companies for which I have not completed at least ten assignments. Sometimes I may stretch this to twelve to fifteen assignments.

There will also be companies, which offer such strong benefits in terms of food, service, entertainment, or products, that you will most likely find yourself quite willing to take less than a dollar a minute for your work. The fine dining experiences are a good example. Fine dining assignments usually pay between $20 and $40 per assignment. If I were paid the average—$30 for a fine dining assignment—that would mean that to make a dollar a minute, I would have to get into the restaurant, consume a great meal, and get out in thirty minutes. That simply will not happen; nor do I want it to. I tell all the companies I work for that I will accept all the fine dining assignments they wish to give me, and I won't watch the clock. In fact, my wife and I often spend up to three hours eating and drinking at a fine dining restaurant and get paid $25, $30, or $35 for writing the report. However, the bill for which I am totally reimbursed will rarely be under $100, and it sometimes exceeds $200.

Fortunately, a growing number of mystery shopping companies pay well and also provide good products or services. For example, one company asks shoppers to complete a ten-question check-off questionnaire after shopping in the stores of one of its clients. The budget for the item shopped is $20. Average shopping time is usually no more than four or five minutes, and the pay for writing the report is a standard $15. If you spend four minutes shopping and one minute filling out the questionnaire, your total time expenditure is five minutes. The income is $3 a minute, and the product you keep is worth $4 a minute. The total comes to $7 per minute or $420 per hour. Most would agree. That is excellent compensation for any job.

A MILLION DOLLARS FROM MYSTERY SHOPPING

Setting goals and working toward those goals can be as effective with mystery shopping as with any other employment vehicle one wishes to use to accumulate wealth. As with any part-time job, much depends on what you do with the money you earn. If one considers that the income from mystery shopping is "add-on" money—money that you would not have if you were not working at a "second" or "add-on" job—then the next logical step in the reasoning process is that you should not count on this money to maintain your lifestyle. One way to avoid the trap of living up to the combination of your full-time and your add-on income, i.e., spending the income from your part-time job as rapidly as spending the income from your full-time job, is to simply put the money from your add-on job (the money paid to you for writing mystery shopping reports) into a bank account. If that money is invested wisely as it accumulates, it can provide a nice long-term lifestyle that is likely to be much better than you might have imagined.

Several years ago Amy Gand wrote me saying that

she had decided to save and invest all income earned as a mystery shopper. At the time of her writing, she was earning several hundred dollars a month as a part-time mystery shopper. She said if she continued to save and invest her income from mystery shopping and the investment interest on earned income stayed the same or went up, she would be a millionaire by the time she retired, according to her calculations. Not everyone has the discipline or determination that Amy has, but it is nice to know that mystery shopping has the potential to make a person a millionaire.

SAYING "NO" IS OKAY

As noted earlier, mystery shopping is one of the few jobs where it is okay to say, "no." Although it is seldom wise to turn down a first assignment from a mystery shopping company, once you have conducted several shopping assignments with most companies, the person who works for the shopping company making assignments (usually called the assignment giver) will understand and will not hold it against you if you turn down one or more assignments.

Everyone understands that this is a part-time job. Therefore, if the assignment has to be completed during the hours you are working full-time, you will not be expected to risk problems with your full-time employer by taking off to complete a mystery shopping assignment. Similarly, if you have a vacation trip planned, a doctor's appointment, or some other prescheduled activity for which you have already made a commitment, mystery shopping company executives will not expect you to break a commitment to undertake a mystery shopping assignment. And if you turn down an assignment because the pay is too low, most shopping company executives will make a note not to call you again for the lower-paying assignments, but if your past work with the company has been good, they will make a computer file note to call you for assignments that pay what you tell them you must receive (or more). And, they will respect you for your professionalism.

There are other reasons why you might want to say "no," however, and if you explain your position, shopping company executives will understand and will not ask you to undertake such assignments. One of the reasons in this category has to do with risk. Some shoppers do not want to undertake any assignment that might have any degree of risk.

For example, the Saturday morning security guard check, which was described in chapter 1, is the type of assignment that some shoppers won't undertake because of risk. One elderly lady said, "The security guard carries a gun. He might shoot me!" Although it is doubtful that the shopper would be shot, shopping company executives will understand if you indicate that you will not undertake such an assignment because you consider it risky. They will find another shopper who will take the assignment.

A second type of assignment that some shoppers say "no" to really can entail some degree of risk. Often the stores shopped are convenience stores. This type of shopping assignment was noted in the last chapter in the section on honesty and theft prevention shopping. It is possible that a convenience store clerk might think you are a mystery shopper and might fear losing his job or being arrested if he thinks you have witnessed his stealing the change you left when paying for a candy bar or newspaper. And under these circumstances, the clerk might come after you. Some shoppers are not afraid of the potential repercussions and take on these assignments because they pay well. Other shoppers will not consider taking on such risky assignments. As with security shops, however, it is okay to turn down this type of assignment. And if you explain that you are concerned about the risk, the assignment giver will note your concern and will not call you again with such an assignment. Here again, saying "no" will not stop you from getting future assignments that are less risky.

Still another reason to say "no" is embarrassment. Some men are uncomfortable buying clothes for women. Even married men who buy nice evening clothes for their wives may feel uncomfortable when buying other items of women's clothing. This is especially true when it comes to lingerie. But when a shopping company executive signs a contract to do lingerie shops, the client company will often ask that a certain percentage of the shoppers should be men. To get men to undertake such assignments, it is not unusual for the shopping company to offer better pay than they might otherwise be willing to pay. Nevertheless, many men will not undertake such a shopping assignment no matter how much they are paid. And, while they would prefer that it would be otherwise, shopping company executives will understand and (reluctantly) accept it if the male shopper declines this type of shopping assignment.

But while it is okay to say "no" to shopping assignments, it should be remembered that the assignments that are turned down are often the assignments that pay the best. If you want to make real money as a mystery shopper, carefully consider before you say "no."

DON'T KEEP THE CAR

One of the things people most like about mystery shopping is being able to keep the things they purchase. However, most companies have contracts calling for some of their mystery shoppers to *not* complete the purchase specifically so that they will not keep the item. In these cases, the buying process is brought right up to the actual purchase and then the buyer (mystery shopper) backs off. New car shops are an example of this (see chapter 1). Many automobile dealerships want to know how well their sales people are interacting with clients. But they do not want to give away a new car each time they are shopped. Therefore, in the case of new car shops, expect to receive a written notice in your paperwork, which states: "DO NOT KEEP THE CAR." Another example is real estate. One is not expected to buy a house or to sign a lease on an apartment.

In most cases, when the mystery shopper is told to not actually purchase the item for which he or she has shopped, mystery shopping companies know that the shopper is getting less than he or she would when shopping for something that could be kept or consumed. Therefore, the average pay for these assignments tends to be better than for those assignments during or after which one can keep or consume the items purchased. The pay tends to be from $5 to $15 greater per assignment than for those assignments in which the item purchased may be consumed or kept.

ADDITIONAL INCOME SOURCES

The pay mystery shoppers receive for writing shopping reports constitutes the vast majority of income mystery shoppers get as compensation for their work. It is such a substantial part that many shoppers ignore or pay no attention to other "additional" sources of income. But as they say, "Every penny counts." It is wise to consider the fact that returns can pay as much as twice what a single purchase will pay. Mileage can add up—especially when it is used as an area of negotiation. And fax expense compensation can add up over a period of time. Negotiations, however, can give an experienced shopper a much greater annual income than is garnered by a shopper who never negotiates. Therefore, it is suggested that all additional income sources be sought and considered when deciding what companies to work with and what assignments to take.

RETURNS Mystery shopping company assignment givers will sometimes ask the mystery shopper to return the item or items purchased. They realize that this involves two shopping trips and the writing of two shopping reports. Because of the additional work and because the shopper is unable to keep the product, this type of assignment tends to be well paying. Most companies requiring returns will pay the mystery shopper twice the amount of the money paid for the initial shopping experience. There are not many that require a product return. However, many mystery shoppers jump at the chance to do shopping assignments that include a return. The return report form tends to be short, as does the time spent returning an item at the store. The end result winds up being good pay for a small amount of additional time. If you like doing returns—and the money that goes with them—tell the assignment giver. It would probably not be wise to ask for an assignment calling for a return during one of your first four or five assignments with a company, but once you have completed assignments and especially once you have established a good rapport with your assignment giver (the person who calls to give you assignments), ask for an assignment that involves returning the item. After you have tried it once, if you like the pay, tell the assignment giver that you would like as many of these assignments as he or she has in your area.

MILEAGE Most mystery shopping companies will not pay for the shopper's driving or "mileage" costs. However, a few companies do offer a mileage compensation. This tends to range from twenty-five cents per mile to forty-five cents per mile. You will be expected to track your mileage and to report it on an expense report form. Simply log in the odometer reading on your car before leaving your house. Enter the reading

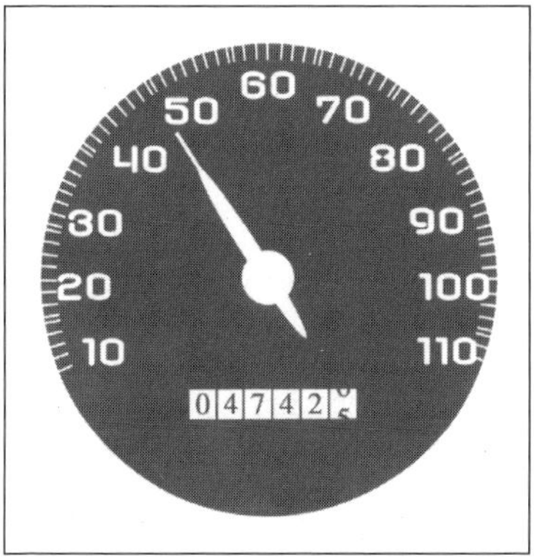

on your report form when you arrive at the shopping location and again enter the reading when you get back home. To calculate your mileage compensation, subtract the odometer reading taken at the beginning of the trip from the reading taken at the end when you return home. The result will be the total miles driven. Multiply this times the rate per mile agreed to by the mystery shopping company. The result will be the dollar compensation amount to be entered on your expense report form.

FAX EXPENSE COMPENSATION Timeliness is important. Therefore, a few companies will ask you to fax your shopping reports to them. Usually when this is requested, the mystery shopping company will compensate you for a reasonable per page faxing cost. It would be a good idea to compare fax costs at office supply and fast print companies in your neighborhood. The costs tend to range from less than $1 per page (not including the cover page) to over $8 per page (including the cover page). Some mystery shopping companies compensate actual costs (include your receipt) up to a budgeted per page total. The mystery shopping company assignment giver may ask you what it will cost to fax your report. If you have already comparison-shopped your neighborhood, you will know what the per page cost will be when asked on the phone.

NEGOTIATE Sometimes mystery shopping company executives will be caught in a bind. They will ask you to go a long distance to complete a shopping assignment, help in covering a last-minute assignment situation, or complete an assignment that for some reason no one else will take. Because they are asking for something that goes beyond the normal, the mystery shopping executive will often offer more money than one would usually be paid.

It is important to understand why these situations occur and to put them into perspective. When a mystery shopping company client signs a contract with a mystery shopping company, it usually calls for having each department of each store or branch in the chain shopped on a regular basis (usually once a month). If it is a small regional specialty store chain, there may only be ten or fifteen stores in a two or three state area and the contract may only call for one shopping assignment per store each month, i.e., ten or fifteen shops per month. However, if it is a large international department store chain with four hundred stores throughout the United States and Canada, the contract may call for two thousand or more shops each month. Each department of each store will need to be shopped each month. Typically, the contract calls for the mystery shopping company to pay a penalty if any store or department is not shopped when it should be. The penalty may be as much as $50 to $100 per department or store per day for any scheduled mystery shopping assignment that is missed. In addition, a large number of contracts call for the entire mystery shopping contract with the client to be cancelled if too many scheduled mystery shopping assignments are not completed or not completed on time.

A couple of examples will illustrate what might be involved. A shopper was called with a request that she complete an assignment in a smaller town more than seventy-five miles away. The shopping company executive explained that he had tried to find a shopper in the smaller town for three months, ever since the contract with his client company had been signed. He took out advertisements in the classified section of the local newspaper. There were no responses, and he failed to get the client's store in that city shopped. The client was upset and penalized the mystery shopping company with the agreed-upon monetary penalty.

During the second month, newspaper advertising failed to find a mystery shopper, so toward the end of the month the mystery shopping executive contracted with a temporary agency in the small town and the agency sent one of its people in to mystery shop the client's store. However, the report filed with the client company was so bad that the client company refused to accept it, invoked a financial penalty to be paid by the mystery shopping company, and told the owner of the mystery shopping company that the entire contact would be cancelled if the store in the smaller town did not get shopped and a quality report provided the next month. It was toward the end of the third month when the mystery shopping company executive contacted the shopper who lived seventy-five miles away. He offered to pay anything within reason if the experienced mystery shopper would drive the seventy-five miles, complete a shopping report (all of the reports of this shopper are of top quality), and get the report in well before the end of the month.

The lingerie example in the previous chapter is another example of a situation in which the mystery shopping company faced paying a substantial penalty unless it could find a shopper to cover the assignment.

But the most common emergency coverage

situation occurs when a shopper fails to complete an assignment on time. The shopper to whom the assignment was given becomes ill, moves to another city, dies, or perhaps just decides not to complete the assignment. If the shopper who was originally given the assignment calls and says he or she will miss the assignment because of illness, death in the family, etc. then the mystery shopping company executive may be pushed to find another shopper, but will often have a few days in which to locate a new shopper. However, if the shopper decides not to complete the assignment she was given and does not inform the mystery shopping company, the company executive probably won't be alerted to the situation until well after the report was due—which is late in the game. In such an event, the mystery shopping executive will need to get the job reassigned immediately.

Every month, mystery shopping companies scramble to find good shoppers fast to meet their contractual obligations. In many cases, they will offer the shopper more money if the shopper will take on the assignment—usually right away. Under these circumstances, mystery shoppers should feel comfortable to negotiate. If you must cancel other scheduled activities to drive seventy-five miles to complete an assignment the next day, you may feel you should receive more in additional compensation than the mystery shopping executive first offers. It is unwise to take advantage of the mystery shopping company when it has a problem, but at the same time, you need to feel that you are adequately compensated for taking care of an emergency situation. It is usually better to negotiate a compensation you will be comfortable with rather than just turn down the initial offer. Remember, however, that if you are willing to take a reasonable compensation for your extra effort, most mystery shopping executives will remember that you helped out in an emergency and will try to make it up to you by giving you more of their "better" assignments.

TAX CONSIDERATIONS Most mystery shopping companies will hire you on an assignment-by-assignment basis as an independent contractor. This means that they will not deduct taxes from the compensation paid to you. In fact, unless you have a large number of assignments from them, they will not send you an end-of-year report of the amount of money paid to you (on an IRS 1099 form). Tracking your income will be your responsibility, and paying taxes on that income is also your responsibility. Many people who do only a small amount of mystery shopping simply ask their main employer to reduce their deductions by one person. This means that the main employer sends the government more money than needed for the income paid by them. Ideally, the additional money sent by your main employer will offset the lack of any money sent by you for your mystery shopping work. If so, this will result in your not owing more taxes at the end of the year.

The Internal Revenue Service holds each American responsible for paying his or her taxes. If the employer does not deduct taxes (and mystery shopping companies that work with you as an independent contractor do not deduct taxes), the taxpayer is responsible for sending tax payments to the IRS each quarter (every three months). If you earn several hundred dollars per month on mystery shopping (a large number of mystery shoppers earn this much and more) or if you are already claiming zero deductions, check with your accountant or bookkeeper to set up arrangements for sending quarterly tax payments to the Internal Revenue Service. In your first year, it will probably be only a small amount of money you will need to send each quarter. The cost of a bookkeeper to set up the IRS account system for you will also be small. However, since the process of setting it up is so simple, many mystery shoppers set up their quarterly tax payment systems themselves. Call your local IRS office and ask them to send you the forms and the set of instructions that spell out how to complete the forms.

AVOID CREDIT CARD DEBT ACCUMULATION

Most mystery shopping purchases are made by credit card. This means that mystery shoppers can accumulate substantial balances on their credit card accounts. Fortunately, mystery shopping company executives know that mystery shoppers do not want to pay interest on the amount owed to the credit card company for mystery shopping purchases. Therefore, most mystery shopping companies send checks to mystery shoppers every four weeks. These are lump sum checks. In other words, one check will cover all mystery shopping purchases, all expense report compensation, and all shopping report compensation due to the mystery shopper since the last check was cut (usually one month ago). Mystery shoppers usually get the monthly check well before credit card balances for those items purchased during the month need to be paid. In other words, mystery shoppers can expect to receive the money to pay for mystery shopping purchases before the credit card deadline for purchase payment is due.

When a person is mystery shopping on a large-scale basis, however, establishing a credit card just for mystery shopping purchases can be a good idea. If this is done, then opening a bank account solely for mystery shopping company checks to be deposited in (and the credit card payment check to be written on) can reduce paperwork and can help to reduce or avoid the possibility of credit card debt accumulation.

FIVE WORDS THAT WILL MAKE MONEY FOR YOU

As this chapter clearly points out, mystery shoppers can either make enough to have a nice add-on income or they can make a much greater amount of money. In the last chapter of this book, you will be shown how to parlay an initial toe dip in the waters of mystery shopping into a substantial income by following a set of specific steps. However, even if you do not enter this field with the goal of making several thousand dollars a month from it, you will benefit by memorizing five small words and using them at the appropriate time. Many find that these few simple words can double or triple their income from mystery shopping.

The words are simply, “What else do you have?” To understand how they can help you, consider the case of Jennifer Patrick. Jennifer took a course on mystery shopping on a Saturday evening in April 1995 in Wichita, Kansas. Although she learned in the course that people who are new to mystery shopping are expected to send a letter to mystery shopping companies asking for assignments with them, wait for a set of employment forms to be sent to them, complete the employment forms, and send them back before expecting to get any assignments, Jennifer was motivated by the course and anxious to get started. She purchased a copy of the first edition of this book while attending the course. The next day, Sunday, Jennifer started calling the mystery shopping companies listed in the book. Since it was Sunday, she knew that the companies would be closed and that she would probably not get an answer when she called—and she was right.

However, on the twelfth or thirteenth call, a man answered. She told him she had taken a mystery shopping course the evening before and even though she had not sent a letter asking for work with his company, she would like to get an assignment as soon as possible. The man told Jennifer that he normally was not in the office on Sunday, but it was his job to give out assignments. He explained that when his company contracted to provide mystery shopping, the client expected to have someone shop each of their outlets or branches throughout the country at least once a month and with some clients the shopping frequency was as much as once a week. He told her he had not given out all of last week's assignments to shoppers by Friday afternoon. Therefore, he was in the office calling shoppers trying to finish with all of last week's assignments. He knew that the next morning (Monday) he would receive next week's assignments (several hundred of them), and therefore, he would have to finish giving out last week's assignments that day (Sunday) or he would be hopelessly behind.

Even though Jennifer had not followed the required application process, the mystery shopping company executive agreed to give her an assignment because he knew the quality of her training (and he also was in a bind). He volunteered to enclose with the shopping assignment forms an application form and the other forms needed by the company for Jennifer to get "on file" with his company.

Jennifer thanked him and was ready to hang up when she remembered those magic five little words. And she said, "What else do you have?" He came up with another assignment. After getting the information on that assignment, Jennifer again asked, "What else do you have?" Each time she got an assignment, before she would terminate the phone call, she would ask, "What else do you have?" Finally, the man had no more assignments for Jennifer. She had been given six assignments—all that he had in Wichita. But she got more the next month.

After telling Jennifer that he had no more assignments in Wichita, the man thanked Jennifer. He said that because she had taken so many assignments, he would be able to go home early. Unfortunately, there is an attitude prevalent in the mystery shopping industry about multiple assignments. Mystery shopping company assignment givers (those individuals who call to ask shoppers to take an assignment) tend to believe mystery shoppers do not want more than one assignment at a time, so they don't normally offer more than one assignment per phone call. Mystery shoppers, on the other hand, tend to believe that they will not be given more than one mystery shopping assignment per phone call, so they rarely ask for more than one.

Try asking for multiple assignments. You will like the results. Whenever you speak with a person from a mystery shopping company who asks you to take on a shopping assignment, before you hang up ask, "What else do you have?" And if you get another assignment, ask again—and again. Even if you say "no" to an assignment that is offered, you can often still get another assignment (or two or three or more) if you will simply slip in those wealth-accumulating five words before you hang up. And as you take more and more assignments, think how good it is of you to take so many assignments. Because you are willing to take a large number of assignments, perhaps the person you are talking with on the phone will also be able to go home early.

CHAPTER 3

WHAT A SHOPPER ACTUALLY DOES

The Job Process

Mystery shopping companies usually follow a standard job process. It starts with shoppers being contacted either by phone or by mail (a postcard). Most companies employ people to call mystery shoppers and ask each shopper if he or she is interested in carrying out a shopping assignment during the next few weeks. If the shopper agrees, details of when and how the shopping assignment should be carried out are reviewed on the phone. Reporting requirements are discussed, and compensation is explained.

A few days after the phone conversation, if the shopper has agreed to undertake the shopping assignment, a set of documents will be sent to the shopper. Typically these will include a shopping assignment form providing written confirmation of when the shopping assignment should be undertaken (see figure 3.1, Two Examples of Shopping Schedule and Instruction Sheets) and when the shopping report should be mailed or faxed to the mystery shopping company. The assignment form will also have the address of the place to be shopped, and it will usually include a phone number to call if reservations (for a restaurant shop, a beauty shop appointment, or some other service type of assignment) need to be made or if the shopper needs to call to get driving directions (perhaps to ask where the nearest major cross streets are). The package will include a customer service evaluation form (a blank shopping report form—see figure 3.2, Example of a Shopping Report), and it will sometimes include special notes.

The mystery shopper is expected to review all print materials received and confirm that the written materials agree with the details both parties agreed to over the phone. The shopper is then expected to conduct the shopping assignment in accordance with the instructions and within the time frame provided by the mystery shopping company. Then the mystery shopper is expected to complete the evaluation (shopping report) form. The shopper mails, faxes, or overnight expresses the shopping report, the expense report (if appropriate), and receipts (if appropriate) to the mystery shopping company; this also usually includes a bill for his or her services. A few weeks later, the mystery shopping company sends the mystery shopper a check to compensate for completing the mystery shopping assignment and to reimburse the shopper for whatever was purchased.

IT STARTS WITH A PHONE CALL

Mystery shopping companies usually start the job assignment process by making a phone call. You, the mystery shopper, may receive the call at any hour of the business day or during evening hours. Because you never know when the call will come, it is wise to have an answering machine. Most company executives will leave a message if you are not at home to receive their call. You should, however, call back as soon as possible as company executives (assignment givers) work an assignment list consistently until all assignments are made.

Because mystery shopping executives know that most shoppers are part-time independent contractors and that the majority of mystery shoppers have full-time jobs, a large number of the mystery shopping companies employ assignment givers (those individuals who make phone calls to offer assignments to mystery shoppers) who work evenings and weekends. They know that the majority of people who work on a full-time basis work from 8 a.m. (local time) to 6 p.m. (local time) from Monday through Friday. Therefore, during the workweek, most calls are made between 5:30 p.m. and 9:30 p.m. local time, and during weekends, most calls are made between 8:30 a.m. and 5 p.m.

Some companies will send a postcard to all shoppers who have worked with them in the past (see figure 3.3, Sample Postcard Advising Assignment Request Schedule). This card typically provides dates for shoppers to call based on the first letter of the last name of the shopper. For example, it might say, "Please call from 8 a.m. to 5 p.m. Eastern Standard Time on the following dates in May to get June shopping assignments: May 03 … H-O; May 04 … P-Z; May 05 … A-G". Frequently, a toll-free 800 number is provided for shoppers.

When you speak with the assignment giver, you will

FIGURE 3.1 Example of a Shopping Schedule and Instruction Sheet

Shopper No. 286

July

Instructions on the back

STORE NO.	12 to 7PM 1st through 7th	3 to 7PM 8th through 14th	12 to 7PM 15th through 21st	3 to 7PM 22st through 27th	12 to 7PM through 28th
10					
11			286		
12					
13					
14					
15				281	
16					
17		188			
18					
1					
2					
3					
4					
5	174				
6					
7					

National Shopping Service Network, LLC 6/01/95

FIGURE 3.1 Example of a Shopping Schedule and Instruction Sheet

HOTEL

Number: __________ You have __________Shops

Breakfast Buffet that is presented in the

INSTRUCTIONS

Please type or print very clearly in black ink. Make an appropriate comment at each opportunity to do so.

The primary purpose of the shop is to check integrity. However, Customer service will be checked too, while we are there.

Go prepared to pay cash.

Both the shopper and guest are to order the BREAKFAST BUFFET.

It is possible that some of the wait staff is presenting the same guest check to more than one patron.

Be sure to record the serial number on the guest check that is presented to you. But DO NOT tear the stub off the guest check. When your guest check is presented, put enough cash in the tray with the check to cover the amount as well as the tip. If possible, leave all this on the table and GO. Don't wait for change. And again, be sure to leave the guest check intact.

If you have any questions at all, please call Howard.

Pays $15.00 plus reimbursement of expenses for and parking for shopper & 1 guest.

Mail to:

SHOP THIS DATE:	WHEN TO BE THERE:	SHOP	Shopper No:
	7:15 AM	BREAKFAST BUFFET	
	8:15 AM	BREAKFAST BUFFET	

National Shopping Service Network, LLC.

FIGURE 3.2 Example of a Shopping Report

HOTEL

A CUSTOMER SERVICE AND INTEGRITY AUDIT

Restaurant Bill $12.83
Tip 1.67
Valet Parking 8.00
Parking Tip in 1.00
Parking Tip out 1.00

Address: ______ Shopper No. 286

Guest Check # 255969 Total Expense $ $24.50

Day: Monday Date: 17 July Time: In 8:15 am Seated: 8:16 am Out: 8:55 a.m.

Weather: Sunny,warm,74° Percent seats occupied at Restaurant: 85%-90%

Host/Hostess name & description: Mike,6'1" tall appox, blond, late 20s to early 30s, Mike wore a full apron tied behind his neck and around his waist.

Server name & description: David, about 5'10" tall, black hair - long in back, but not to his shoulders, a heavy black mustache, dark tan, about mid to late 20s, black slacks, gray shirt, apron tied at waist, but not at the top

Manager(s) names & descriptions: Mike, the same person who seated us. Mike was at the cashier's desk when we arrived and worked from that station

SCORE: 0 = No or unacceptable 2 = Average 3 = Yes or Excellent

Calculate a Percentage Score: ______ / ______ ( ) ______ %

CUSTOMER SERVICE

1. Who greeted at arrival? Mike, (see above)
   How long before you were greeted? Immediately upon arrival (3) ____
   Describe greeting message: Good morning - Do you want smoking or non-smoking? (3) ____
2. What did host or hostess do & recommend while seating you? He said nothing to us as we went to the table. He pulled out the seat and said our waiter would be with us shortly. (3) ____
3. What was your server's greeting? Good morning! How may I help you, gentlemen? was the server's greeting. (3) ____
4. Did your server project a special sense of enthusiasm, guest awareness and guest importance? Yes X No ____
   How so? He seemed rushed, but used the term, "gentlemen" (3) ____
5. What was done to suggestive sell the bar or an alternate beverage?
   Nothing (3) ____
6. What was done to suggestive sell the Breakfast Buffet?
   There was no effort to sell the buffet. After asking where the buffet was, he described the foods and their location at the buffet. (3) ____
7. Did the server describe the breakfast buffet? Yes X No ____ (3)
   See comments under number 6 above
8. Was the breakfast buffet well stocked? Yes X No ____ (3)
9. Was the breakfast buffet fresh & attractive? Yes X No ____ (3)
10. Was the buffet clean and free of spills? Yes ____ No X (3)
11. Were the food items on the buffet labelled? Yes ____ No X (3)
12. Plate warmer had an ample supply of plates? Yes X No ____ (3)
13. Warm plates were available? Yes ____ No X (3)
14. Did the server offer appropriate condiments? Yes ____ No X (3)
15. Did server check back in a timely fashion? Yes X No ____ (3)

National Shopping Service Network, LLC

FIGURE 3.2 Example of a Shopping Report

Comments on any "No" answers to Questions 9 through 15.

Q10 There were a few small spills, nothing major.
Q11 None were labelled.
Q13 There were enough plates available, but none were warmed.
Q14 David, the server, offered no condiments. However, when asked for catsup, he brought a bottle right away.

16. Rate the Work habits of the Crew: Correctly completing tasks, no lounging, eating or hanging out with off duty employees. Circle appropriate:
Poor (0) (2) (3) (Excellent:) (3) ______
17. Guest check number: 255969
18. All items were rung on the guest check? Yes X No ____ (3) ______
We were charged for a child's meal even though I told David my son is over 12.
19. Who presented guest check? (name if possible, & description)
The server, David (for description, see top of page one)
20. Who picked it & money up? (name if possible, & description)
David (see description at the top of page one)
21. "All" cash handling seemed to be appropriate: Yes X No ____ (3) ______
Comment: David asked if he could take the payment. I said "yes", and he took both the money and the bill.

FOOD QUALITY

List what was selected and tell how it was:

Presentation, taste and temperature

22.

ITEM	PRESENTATION	TASTE	TEMPERATURE
Sausage	Good	good	Okay
Bacon	Good	good	good
Scrambled eggs	Good	Okay	Too cool
~~Rice Krispy Cereal~~	~~Good~~	~~good~~	~~good~~
Doughnut	Good	good	good
Waffle	Good	good	good
Omlet (There was a long wait for	Good	good	good
~~Potatoes~~	~~Good~~	~~good~~	~~good~~
Bacon	Good	good	good
Yogurt (The selection was small & hard to find	Good	good	good

Further evaluate the meals by circling the appropriate number:

Received what was ordered:	Poor	0	2	(3)	Excellent	(xx 6)	____
Hot food hot & cold food cold:	Poor	0	2	(3)	Excellent	(xx 6)	____
Appearance/Presentation	Poor	0	2	(3)	Excellent	(xx 6)	____
Taste:	Poor	0	2	(3)	Excellent	(xx 6)	____

National Shopping Service Network, LLC

FIGURE 3.2 Example of a Shopping Report

23. Rate each on interior appearance: Poor 0 2 3 Excellent
Entrance/Waiting area _X_ Booths N/A Tables _3_
Walls _3_ Ceiling _3_ Floors/Carpet _3_ Chairs _3_ (27) ____
Menu was neat, clean and in good condition _3_
Reasons for anything less than 3: N/A

24. Rate each of the following: Poor 0 2 3 Excellent
Table top condiments set ups _3_ Plates _3_ Flatware _3_
Glassware _3_ Waitstaff uniforms _3_ Tables _3_
Chairs _3_ Floor/Carpet _3_ All employees were clean & well groomed _3_ Temperature "comfortable" _3_ (30) ____
Reasons for anything less than 3:

25. Rate the restroom for cleanliness: Men's _3_ Women's N/A
Smells/Dirty 0 2 3 Neat/Clean
Reasons for anything less than 3: (3) ____

26. Was the restroom well-stocked with soap, toilet paper, towels, working hand dryers and all fixtures functional?
Yes _X_ No ____ Reasons for anything less than 3: (3) ____

27. Rate the Health Consciousness of the Staff: Good sanitation habits being practiced by everyone. Yes _X_ No ____
Comments: (9) ____

KEY QUESTIONS

28. Describe what you saw with regard to the use or re-use of Guest Checks that were created and presented to you and the other patrons.
There was nothing to indicate that this guest check had been used before.

29. Who of the staff would you choose as STAR EMPLOYEES? Who and Why?
Mike, the manager, was constantly on the move. The restaurant was very busy, but he got people seated rapidly and handled questions smoothly. He kept track of staff members and quietly directed a very busy restaurant calmly and professionally.

FIGURE 3.2 Example of a Shopping Report

30. Rate your overall experience up to 100%.
What grade do you award? 98%
Why do you feel your rating is appropriate?
The quality and easy handling of a large number of people is hard to do. No patron seemed to have any problem that was not taken care of right away. There was a variety of food and it was set out in such a way that there were no long lines. The food was well-prepared and generally it was well presented.

FURTHER INFORMATION

Provide any further information of importance, reference by question number when appropriate.

National Shopping Service Network, LLC

be advised as to when (day and time requirements) the shopping assignment needs to be undertaken, where the store or restaurant to be shopped is located, what item or items you will be expected to shop for, when the shopping report will be due, and how much the shopping assignment will pay. Additionally, you may or may not be advised regarding expense compensation (what expenses will be and will not be covered), and you may be given instructions specific to the new shopping assignment. If you are not sure about something, this is the time to ask questions. If for some reason you do not want to accept the shopping assignment, say so and give the shopping executive your reasons for rejecting the assignment. If your reason is at all reasonable, you can expect to be offered another assignment with the company. Sometimes, you will get another assignment offer during the same phone call—especially if you remember those important words, "What else do you have?" If not, you may have to wait a few days for the next round of assignment calls.

COMPUTER CONTACTS AND COMPUTER ASSIGNMENTS

In recent years, an increasing number of mystery shopping companies have computerized their process of hiring mystery shoppers, providing mystery shopping assignments, preparing mystery shopping reports, and filing mystery shopping reports. Some companies refuse to work with mystery shoppers who do not have home computers with Internet access. Although rare, a few also require the shoppers with whom they work to have home fax machines and dedicated phone lines. The National Shopping Service Network (NSSN) has sophisticated the computerized interrelationship with

FIGURE 3.3 Sample Postcard Advertising Assignment Request Schedule

Call Schedule

Please call to schedule shopping assignments during the following times and dates. The schedule is based on the first letter of your last name. Please call from 8 a.m. to 5 p.m. Eastern Standard Time on the following dates in MAY to get JUNE shopping assignments.

May 03	H-0
May 04	P-Z
May 05	A-G

A toll-free number has been provided for your convenience. The number is 1-800-123-4567.

mystery shoppers to the point that the only non-computer contact for most of its assignments is the issuance of the check for payment. It still comes in the mail. However, the mystery shopping company is working toward electronically transferring payment to the bank accounts of its mystery shoppers.

Most of the mystery shopping companies that work with shoppers via the Internet will have home pages on which mystery shopper applications are displayed. The shopper is expected to complete the application online and to send it to the mystery shopping company by pressing the "SEND" button once the application has been completed. Some of these companies will include other forms (in addition to the application form), which must be completed online and returned online. Typically, once an application has been approved by the mystery shopping company, the mystery shopper is given an access code. Using the code, the new mystery shopper may access a listing of "open" assignments (those assignments that have not yet been taken by other mystery shoppers). Frequently assignments are grouped geographically. In other words, shoppers look for assignments in their state, province, or territory by going down the alphabetical listing of states, provinces, and territories. Then they look for their city or town in an alphabetical listing by city/town. Finally, some mystery shopping companies will categorize assignments by zip or postal code.

Once a computer-generated assignment has been received, it is wise to print a "hard" copy of the mystery shopping report form. Fill out this hard copy form after completing the shopping assignment. Then either transfer the data to the online shopping report form and electronically send it back to the mystery shopping company or, using a scanner, capture the hard copy data on your computer and electronically send it back. If you have a home-based fax machine, many mystery shopping companies will allow you to fax the completed hard copy form to the mystery shopping company.

For more detailed information on computerized mystery shopping and a discussion of individual mystery shopping companies that work with mystery shoppers via computer, go to the section titled, "Computer-Based Mystery Shopping Companies" in chapter 6.

THE CALENDAR VISIT REPORT ENTRY

The number one complaint mystery shopping companies have about new mystery shoppers and the number one reason why some mystery shoppers are terminated after their first assignment is failure to complete the shopping assignment on schedule and/or failure to complete the shopping report and get it to the mystery shopping company on time. Those new to mystery shopping are particularly susceptible to treating shopping deadlines in a cavalier manner.

To understand why the deadlines are so important, consider the case of the restaurant owner who pays his entire staff to come in on Monday mornings for the weekly staff meeting (this was discussed at the end of chapter 1). The entire meeting is centered on the mystery shopping reports for shops conducted during the previous week. If all six mystery shoppers assigned to his restaurant adhered to their own deadlines and failed to meet the client's deadlines, the restaurant owner would find himself in the position of paying his entire staff to come in for a meeting with no agenda, i.e., no mystery shopping reports to discuss.

It is because client companies use mystery shopping reports right away that the timeliness is so important. Therefore, always enter the time of the upcoming shop into your calendar. If your calendar is already full, pass on the shopping assignment and ask to be considered for an assignment on a date when you will have more time. Be sure to check your schedule for time to write the report as well. It does no good to complete a shopping assignment on time and then find yourself too busy to complete the shopping report.

THE DOCUMENT PACKAGE

You, the mystery shopper, will receive a document package anywhere from two days to two weeks after you have accepted an assignment. This package will come in the mail, or it will be sent by a private, express-mail service. Be sure to read all items in the package as soon as it arrives, especially the assignment documents and the shopping report that is to be completed. Check to make sure that the date and time on the assignment form(s) match those noted in your calendar when you accepted the assignment on the phone. If there are differences, call the mystery shopping company right away to determine which date/time is accurate—the one received by phone or the one received in the mail. Straighten out any other differences that might be discovered. It is important to do this even if the new date, time, or other requirement discovered when reviewing the documents will work for you. Most of the time differences are slight. You might have heard incorrectly during the phone conversation, or you might have written down the information incorrectly.

MY NAME IS NOT "SUE"

Please keep in mind that the people working with mystery shopping companies are dealing with a mass of assignments and the paperwork related to them. They sometimes make a mistake. One time I received a package in the mail about four days after accepting an assignment on the phone. I opened the package and began to review the documents. The cover sheet had the name of "Sue" on it and had a shopper number that was quite different than my shopper number. That, of course, was a good clue that I had the wrong paperwork. I looked further and confirmed that these papers were not for the assignment I had accepted on the phone. I immediately phoned the mystery shopping company and explained that my name is not "Sue," my shopper number is different than the one on the documents, and the documents appeared to be for an assignment other than the one I had accepted. The assignment giver for the mystery shopping company was able to determine whose set of papers I had right away. It took a little longer, however, for him to find my paperwork. I returned the set of papers I received and, in a few days, received the correct set of papers. Fortunately, because I had reviewed the paperwork as soon as it arrived, Sue was able to get her set of papers in plenty of time to complete her assignment and I was able to get my set in plenty of time as well. Differences, no matter how slight (or major), need to be resolved, and they need to be resolved as soon as they are discovered.

REMAIN CONFIDENTIAL, BUT GET THE ANSWERS

After you have reviewed the questions to be answered in the shopping report, plan how you will obtain the information. Remember that you need to remain a *mystery* shopper—that is, you must not be recognized as the mystery shopper. For lengthy shops with questionnaires that ask for a lot of information, the best way to obtain and keep the information is to use a tape recorder. A mini-cassette recorder kept in the back pocket or purse and attached to a tiny microphone taped to the flap of your purse or worn with a tie clasp holder under a man's tie will provide a verbal record of the shopping experience. Go to Radio Shack or a similar office electronics store and ask for advice. You will be amazed at how little you will have to pay for equipment that will do an excellent job for you.

If the shopping assignment is less involved, but still calls for you to retain more information than you are likely to easily remember, try three-inch-by-five-inch cards cut in half. A man can place five to ten of these cut-up cards in his back pocket without drawing unwanted attention. A woman can easily carry them in her purse. Sometime during the middle of the shopping activity, excuse yourself. Go to the restroom. Pull out one or more of the cards and jot down information that you will need to complete your report. Put the card or cards back into your pocket or purse and return to your shopping.

Many shopping assignments will require so little of your memory that you will not need cards or a tape recorder. Short, ten- or fifteen-question check-off forms can usually be filled out in less than a minute when you return to your car.

GUARD AGAINST MEMORY LOSS

Statistics confirm that the average person forgets over 50 percent of information received about an event within twenty-four hours. Much of that memory loss occurs within the first few hours. Although some shoppers wait until they get home to complete shopping reports, most shoppers find that taking a few minutes to jot down the answers to as many questions on the shopping report as possible immediately after returning to their cars after completing shopping assignments is the best way to make sure nothing critical is forgotten (unless you recorded the shopping experience). It's a good idea to make a copy of the shopping report form when you receive it. Leave the copy in your car while you shop. As soon as you get back to the car, jot down a few notes to yourself in all blocks of the report where information is requested which might be forgotten. You will find that completing the original copy of the shopping report (the one that will be mailed to the shopping company) will be much easier with the set of notes you put together right after completing the shopping assignment.

GET ALL THE INFORMATION AND MAKE SURE IT IS ACCURATE

One of the biggest complaints mystery shopping executives have of mystery shoppers is that the shopper leaves sections of the shopping report blank. Shoppers are paid to get *all* the information. Therefore, it is imperative that all requested information be obtained. If, however, some bit of information has not been obtained, explain in detail why.

Employee names are especially important. The organization being shopped is probably counting heavily on mystery shoppers to provide accurate information about how employees are doing their jobs. They use shopper reports to rate, evaluate, critique, promote, and—yes—fire employees. And they pay a high price to mystery shopping companies for accurate information about the performance of their employees. One mystery shopper was surprised when she received a call from a shopping company executive. The executive had reviewed her most recent report and noted that the shopper had failed to provide the name of the employee who served her. That section had been left blank. The mystery shopper candidly told the executive that she had forgotten to get the name of the employee, but that the employee was an older woman, as noted in the employee description part of the report. The shopper was surprised when the shopping company executive suggested she go back to the store and confidentially get the name of the employee. "Without the name," he said, "your report is useless to us, and unless you get the name, we will be unable to pay you for your work." She returned to the store, bought something, and got the name of the employee as she passed through the checkout counter. When she returned home, the shopper called the mystery shopping company and gave the name to the shopping company executive. The shopper reported that although she, the shopper, had to pay for the cost of driving her car back to the store, pay for the item purchased, and pay for the long-distance call to report back to the shopping company, she felt that correcting her mistake immediately and paying all costs involved in correcting the mistake was what kept her from losing her job with the mystery shopping company.

Sometimes, however, getting all the required information (including the employee's name) is not possible without losing your confidentiality and exposing yourself as a mystery shopper. When this happens, the best thing to do is to clearly explain why you could not obtain the requested information. Detail your reasons in your written report and in a telephone call to your assignment giver.

Once, when shopping, I was unable to get the name of the employee who helped me. However, the assignment form stressed that getting the employee's name was important. The only employee in the store was a young woman who stood behind a high and rather wide counter. She wore her name badge on a chain around her neck. It was a long chain, and the badge hung about one foot directly below her navel. Because of the height and width of the counter, it was impossible to read the name on the badge. I decided that I could climb on the counter and look down, but that I would probably be arrested as a pervert if I did so. When I called and told the shopping executive that I mentally rejected this only feasible way of getting her name, he agreed that my description of the young lady was the best that could be done under the circumstances.

Keep in mind that frequently sales clerks who forget to bring their name badge to work will often look for a badge left behind in the back room and wear it. Therefore, just getting the name is usually not satisfactory. Provide an accurate description of the person as well.

REPORT HONESTLY

A paid mystery shopping assignment is **not** a paid opportunity to get even. Upon receiving an assignment, one person who was new to mystery shopping exclaimed, "This is my time to get even!" She explained that the employees in the store that she was assigned to shop had always treated her rudely, but since it was the only close store of its type, she continued to shop there anyway. However, even if your past experience with the retailer has been totally negative, your evaluation should be an honest report of how the assigned mystery shopping experience took place. If you feel you cannot be unbiased in your reporting, it would be appropriate to point this out when you get a call asking you to mystery shop the store, pass on the assignment, and ask to be considered for an assignment for which you would have no preconceived bias.

SMALL POINTS MAKE A BIG DIFFERENCE

"You are a ceiling man, aren't you?" the company executive asked a mystery shopper. "We like people who report on the condition of ceilings. We have plenty of floor and rug people—and quite a number report on the condition of walls, but we have few ceiling people." This points out one of the values of having several mystery shoppers assigned to shop the same business location. Although all shoppers are expected to report on the small points, we are all individuals. Each of us has our own set of items we think are important. While each shopper answers all questions on the evaluation form, there is room to show your own personality and to indicate what you feel is important.

On a wet, cold November day a mystery shopper who was purchasing an item toward the front of a strip mall store noticed that several people stumbled on a black floor mat placed in front of the door to trap water and ice. No one fell, but the shopper considered the mat a potential hazard and a danger for customers. He indicated his thoughts at the end of the report. A few weeks later, he received a call from the owner of the mystery shopping company. "Thank you," said the owner. "You have garnered us a two-year extension on our contract from the company whose store you shopped in November." The president of the client company read about the mat, flew with his risk management manager to the city where the store was located, investigated, and ordered that the black mats be removed from every store in the chain. A safer, more secure mat was substituted. The president credited the mystery shopping company with saving his retail chain from millions of dollars of potential liability lawsuits. Small points, therefore, make a difference!

TYPED REPORTS ARE USUALLY PREFERRED

Most mystery shopping companies will specify how they want their reports prepared and submitted. The vast majority prefer typed reports. However, few will argue if you have a computer and wish to scan their blank report form into your computer. This will allow you to generate a hard (paper) copy of the report that has been completed on the computer and looks much like a typed copy of the original report. Those with neither a typewriter nor a computer may want to ask for permission to submit the report hand-printed in ink. Many mystery shopping companies, even though they may prefer typed reports, will agree to accept hand-printed reports in ink. Remember, though, that each company is different. One mystery shopping company insists that all of its shoppers submit reports filled out using a number two pencil.

CHAPTER 4

TOOLS OF THE TRADE

No Tools Needed

The vast majority of mystery shoppers do not invest in any special equipment as "tools of the trade" when they get their first assignments. Over a period of time, however, they find that electronic and other devices make their job easier or are required to complete more difficult and better-paying mystery shopping assignments. A few of the more common "tools of the trade" are discussed in this chapter. While you will find that you do not have to have any of these tools to start out as a mystery shopper, you will soon discover that you will want to purchase some of them right away, others later, and some never—unless you decide to undertake specialized types of shopping assignments that may require you to beef up your arsenal of mystery shopping tools.

ANSWERING MACHINE

Owning a good answering machine is almost essential for a mystery shopper. Without one, you run the risk of missing assignments—and money-making opportunities. Although most people have an answering machine or an answering service even before becoming a mystery shopper, if you don't have an answering facility (machine or service) and plan to buy a machine, it is suggested that you purchase a good quality machine. It should be one that has a long message taking ability. A five-minute-per-message capability or longer would be best. Also it should give you the ability to replay individual messages several times. Sometimes you might not pick up a phone number or the details of compensation without having to replay a message two or three times. Finally, look for a machine that will take ten or more messages. You may get several mystery shopping assignment messages within a few hours of one another, and, of course, you will want to pick up and respond to all of these messages. A good electronics store will have several reasonably priced answering machines in stock that will meet all of these criteria.

TYPEWRITER

At one time, almost all mystery shopping companies required reports that were typed. Now far fewer companies require typed reports. In addition, most of the companies that currently require typed reports will also accept computer-generated reports. Therefore, if a shopper has a home computer, he or she will rarely need a typewriter.

Nevertheless, owning a typewriter can be helpful, especially if your hand printing or handwriting is of poor quality. Many short mystery shopping reports can be filled out in the field, i.e., in your car a few minutes after completing a shopping assignment. Mystery shopping executives know that you will not bring a computer or a typewriter in your car with you when you complete a shopping assignment. Therefore, for short reports, they usually accept hand-printed or handwritten reports.

However, for longer reports (three or more pages), printed reports is definitely preferred. In many cases, you can hand-print these reports. But, mystery shopping company executives—and their clients—much prefer typed or computer-generated reports—especially if they are long.

Perhaps the greatest need for a typewriter, however, is to complete mystery shopper application documents. The quality of these documents can make or break your chance of getting assignments with a company for which you have not previously worked. Because mystery shopping companies are selling the reports that mystery shoppers write to their client companies (this is the shopping company's only product), they want to be sure a mystery shopper applicant's paperwork is easily readable and easily understood. When you submit typed application documents, they are easily readable. Therefore, you have increased your competitiveness and your hiring potential.

If you don't own a typewriter but plan to buy one, look for a manual typewriter with a wide carriage. A manual typewriter is preferred for filling out forms because it is easier to set the width on a manual than with an electronic typewriter. A wide carriage allows you to put paper in sideways to fill out document lines that go across the length of the paper.

It can be difficult to find a new typewriter in stores today since typewriters are rapidly being replaced by computers. Estate sales, stores that sell estate sale merchandise, and swap meets offer good opportunities to pick up manual typewriters in good working condition for a small amount of money. Sometimes you can also find one for sale at a pawnshop. One shopper reported she purchased an old typewriter that was still in excellent working condition for only $25 at a store that specializes in selling estate sale merchandise.

HOME COMPUTER

Desktop computers are now found in more than 70 percent of American homes, and Canadians own nearly as many. This, too, is a device that many people own before they become mystery shoppers. Having a computer (desktop or laptop) will open many doors that would otherwise be closed to mystery shopper applicants. In recent years, there has been a strong move by mystery shopping companies to computerize their operations. Now a majority of large regional, national, and international mystery shopping companies will allow mystery shopper applicants to apply online. This means that the shopper applicant may access the home page of the mystery shopping company, go to the mystery shopper applicant section of the Web site, pull up an application form and other application documents, complete them online, and transfer (send) them back to the mystery shopping company online. In other words, the entire application process is completed online, eliminating the need to write a letter asking for application documents, wait for the documents to come, fill out the documents, and mail them back to the mystery shopping company. What would otherwise be about a two-week process (at best) has been

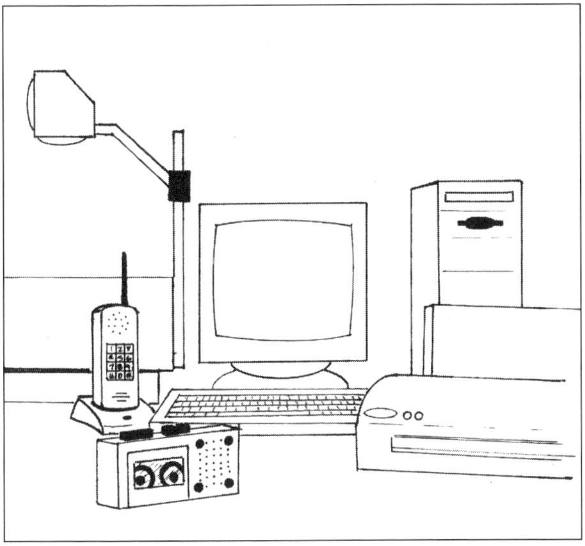

cut down to a thirty- or sixty-minute process. And, with a growing number of mystery shopping companies, applying online is no longer just an option. An increasing number of mystery shopping companies are requiring applications to be completed and filed online and not taking any other type of application.

In addition to being able to apply for mystery shopper positions online, most of the same companies that make online applications possible also provide mystery shopping assignments online. Typically, the mystery shopper is given a "shopper number" and an access code. Using the access code, the shopper is able to review a list of "open" assignments (those that have not been taken by other shoppers) in his or her town or city. The shopper may request one or more of the open assignments. When an assignment is given (allocated) to the mystery shopper, a complete set of shopping assignment documents can be accessed for the assignment. These include a shopping assignment confirmation sheet, a blank shopping report form, and sometimes other forms or documents that need to be completed. One company also provides a map showing where the store/company to be shopped is located. After completing the shopping assignment, the shopper is able to fill out the shopping report online and transfer (send) the completed report back to the mystery shopping company online.

Because so many mystery shopping companies have moved toward this model of working with shoppers, sooner or later the serious mystery shopper embraces the computer application/assignment process. Once a mystery shopper has successfully undertaken applying with a mystery shopping company online and has successfully completed even one shopping assignment online, they rarely look back. They tend to like the online approach and move toward working with many online mystery shopping companies. There are few things as comforting to an experienced mystery shopper as turning on the computer in the morning, going to the e-mail section, and finding multiple messages from mystery shopping companies offering lucrative mystery shopping assignments.

Though most mystery shoppers have desktop computers, a few use laptops. In either case, at the least you will need a CRT (screen or monitor), a computer (the tower or mini-tower that comes with the ensemble), and a printer. If you elect to purchase a laptop, all these components come together in one unit.

In addition to the hardware, you will also need to have Internet capability. This means signing up with an ISP (Internet service provider). This service allows you to access the Web sites of mystery shopping companies and to communicate with those companies online (by using your computer). A dedicated phone line is usually required, but the same line can be shared with a fax machine if you decide you want both.

Finally, you will need to have an e-mail address so that you can receive and send messages. There are several "free" e-mail programs, but most Internet service providers offer better quality e-mail programs at no additional charge, i.e., as a part of their ISP package.

Most office supply stores sell computers, and in major cities, there are many "computer" stores, which specialize in selling computers and computer add-ons. Shop around. Prices and services vary substantially. In each store, tell the salesperson what you want to do with the computer you are considering purchasing. Tell the salesperson that you want to apply for mystery shopping jobs online, communicate with mystery shopping companies online, receive and send mystery shopping reports online, and receive and send both e-mails and e-mail attachments over the Internet. They will be able to recommend equipment and services that will meet your needs, but will be reasonable in cost.

Some of the same stores that sell computer equipment are also Internet service providers. But you do not have to be limited to these firms for Internet service. Turn to your Yellow Pages phone book and look under either "Internet Access Providers" or "Internet Service Providers." Call to check out the range of services and prices. If you want fast, high-quality service and it is available in your area, consider high speed or DSL service. It is several times faster, and also at least twice the cost.

E-mail programs are common inclusions with Internet service. Most ISPs will be able to provide you with a choice of e-mail programs at no cost, and many will be able to offer better e-mail programs at a low cost. While you do not need to get your e-mail program from the ISP provider, it is usually best to do so as e-mail problems are normally either in the program or with the service provider. By having both the e-mail program and the Internet service with the same provider, if something goes wrong, the same firm is responsible no matter where the problem originated.

FAX MACHINE

Some mystery shopping companies ask mystery shoppers to fax their completed mystery shopping reports to the company so that mystery shopping company executives receive your reports as rapidly as possible. And, a few mystery shopping companies require all shoppers who work with them to own a home-based fax machine. If you work with a company that asks for faxed reports, unless they require you to own a machine, you can go to your local office supply house or fast print printer and use their fax at a cost of a few pennies per page. However, if you do much faxing, you may find it more economical and more convenient to own your own fax machine.

You may purchase either a single-function machine or a multifunction machine. The single-function fax machine only provides the ability to receive inbound faxes and to send outbound faxes. It is a simple machine to operate, and it is the least expensive fax machine you can buy. The multifunction machines may also provide the ability to photocopy single-page documents or record voice messages. They may also act as a standard telephone, include a clock, and/or have a tape recorder included. The most important added function, however, is the ability to receive a fax when the shared phone line is tied up while you are connected to the Internet. Then, when you sign off of the Internet and the phone line is free, the stored fax messages will automatically print out on your fax. It is suggested that you forget about all the bells and whistles and get a good quality single-function fax machine with stored fax message capability. If the cost is not much more, you might want to add a single-page copier facility as this can save trips to your local fast print shop for small photocopying needs.

Office product and office equipment stores offer a wide range of single-function and multifunction fax machines. Expect to pay from about $200 to over $500.

SCANNER

A scanner is a timesaving device and nice to have, but it is not necessary in the beginning. A scanner will let you copy a document (or several documents) and put them into your computer. For example, some mystery shoppers want to keep copies of all completed mystery shopping reports so that if a report is lost in the mail, a copy can be sent to the mystery shopping company. If you have a scanner, you can scan each completed mystery shopping report before mailing it to the mystery shopping company. Then if the report is lost in the mail, you can print a copy from your computer and send it to the mystery shopping company by mail, by fax, or as an attachment to an e-mail message.

With scanners, the least expensive is not the best to buy. A scanner needs to be easy to use, of good quality, and able to scan various sized documents so that they reproduce well. You can purchase scanners at computer stores, office supply stores, and office equipment stores.

TAPE RECORDER

One of the biggest problems faced by mystery shoppers is getting all the information and not being able to write it down. A tape recorder fitted with a tiny microphone provides one of the best ways to remain a mystery, but still get all the information.

Fine dining restaurant shops are an excellent example. These shopping assignments usually require the shopper to fill out as many as nine or ten pages of detail, but it is hard to remember every detail before filling out the report. Drinking wine and other drinks before, during, and after dinner also sabotages recall. By wearing a microphone behind a man's tie or having one attached to the flap of a woman's purse, the mystery shopper and the shopper's spouse (or other companion) only need to carry on a conversation while the wait staff is not nearby. They can ask one another such questions as: "Was it Jane or Emily who escorted us to our table?" "Would you agree that she is about 5'8" tall and weighs about 110 pounds?" "Was her hair brown or black?" She had green eyes, didn't she?" "Did it appear to you that the restaurant was full, half full, a quarter full, or almost empty when we were seated for our meal?" "Was it the waiter or the bus person who refilled our water glasses?" Simply by ordering from the menu, you can record data for completing the report. You might say, "I would like a strawberry daiquiri before the meal and my spouse would like a Manhattan—and please serve us the house white zinfandel with dinner."

When you are filling out the mystery shopping report and it asks who escorted you to your table, you can provide the name and a physical description. When the report asks how full the restaurant was, you need only to refer to your recording if you don't remember. You might forget who refilled your water glasses or what you had to drink before and during dinner, but when the report asks for that information, you can rest comfortably knowing that the answer to the question is on the tape.

Many electronic stores offer tape recording systems utilizing hidden microphones. I purchased mine from Radio Shack, but I suggest that you shop around. The cost does not have to be exorbitant. Usually it is no more than $60 to $90.

SPECIAL EQUIPMENT

Some mystery shopping assignments will call for special equipment, but for the vast majority of assignments you will need to bring nothing special with you. If you take on many telephone shopping assignments, you might want to use an over-the-head set of earphones and microphone instead of a standard telephone. Plantronics (www://www.plantronics.com) provides a wide range of over-the-head sets of telephone equipment.

Almost all hotel shopping assignments ask shoppers to report a burned out light bulb. But forcing a light bulb to burn out is a danger you may want to avoid. I bring two burned out light bulbs (of different sizes) with me. You will usually be asked if the carpet in your room was vacuumed, and frequently you will be asked if specific public areas have been vacuumed. My wife saves the lint when washing clothes. She puts it into small plastic bags that I carry with me. I will place tiny amounts of lint in several places in my room and in public rooms and go back later to see if the lint has been vacuumed up.

As you land an increasing number of good mystery shopping assignments, you will find the need to add to your arsenal of equipment to both meet mystery shopping company expectations and to make your job as a mystery shopper easier. You won't need to purchase everything (or even a lot of these items) right away. However, plan to purchase the items you feel you need as you go forward in your career as a mystery shopper. You will find these items will make your work as a mystery shopper easier—and so more enjoyable—over time.

CHAPTER 5

GETTING THE JOB OF MYSTERY SHOPPER

The Job Attainment Process

The job of getting a job as a mystery shopper is one that follows a specific process. It is a process that works. In fact, Elaine Jones from Connecticut reported that she obtained a mystery shopping assignment from the Hilli Dunlap company the day after she finished going through this process. The first step is to identify mystery shopping companies that hire mystery shoppers with no previous experience. This book takes care of the first step for you. Each of the mystery shopping companies listed in this book (see chapter 6, "Mystery Shopping Companies") has been contacted, and an executive from that company has indicated the company does hire people with no experience, i.e., people who have never undertaken mystery shopping assignments in the past.

The second step is to write to mystery shopping

Figure 5.1 A Sample Letter Requesting Employment

Date

Your Name
Street
City/State/Zip Code
Your Contact Phone Number

Name of Contact Person at the Shopping Company (if known)
Title of Contact Person (if known)
Name of Shopping Company
Shopping Company's Address (Street or Box Number)
Shopping Company's City/State/Zip

Dear (Name of Contact Person, if known) [or] (Dear Sir or Madam):

Does your company need a highly qualified mystery shopper in (name of your city/state)? Not only am I an analytical shopper, but I will provide your company with the kind of detailed reports you most likely require. I conduct shopping trips on time—meeting or beating your schedule. And I provide you with a detailed, completed report in 48 hours or less of the shop.

Try my services. You will be happy you did. You can reach me at (your phone number—including area code). If I am not in, please feel free to leave a message. I will get back to you right away.

Sincerely,

Your Name

companies indicating you are interested in working for them as a mystery shopper. This step has also been taken care of for you (see figure 5.1, the Sample Letter Requesting Employment). As will be noted later, it is not recommended that you use this letter exactly as it is presented, but rather it is suggested that you use key phrases and key words from the letter putting them into your own letter structure. The reasons for this will be explained in the section of this chapter addressing the initial contact letter.

After sending a letter asking for employment assignments as a mystery shopper, many companies will send you one or more forms to be completed. These will include some or all of the following: an application form, a shopper profile form, an independent contractor agreement form, and a blank customer service evaluation form (shopping report). They may also ask you to send them your résum´é, but that request is rare. Each of these documents will be discussed in this chapter.

After sending back all required completed documents, follow-up is frequently necessary. This is the final step in the job attainment process. In the list of mystery shopping companies provided in chapter 6, you will no doubt note that company phone numbers are frequently included. However, phone numbers are left out of some of the listings. Where phone numbers are not listed, company executives have specifically asked that their phone numbers not be released. In other words, they either do not encourage phone calls from potential mystery shoppers, or they simply do not want potential mystery shoppers to call them. However, where phone numbers are listed, follow-up

Figure 5-2 A Follow-up Tracking Form

Follow-up Tracking Form

Mystery Shopping Company Name ____________ Contact Executive's Name ____________
Company Address ____________ Contact Executive's Title ____________
____________ Zip ________ Phone Number ____________

STEP BY STEP PROCESS THIS COMPANY USES TO HIRE MYSTERY SHOPPERS

SPECIFIC REQUESTS FROM OR NEEDS OF THIS COMPANY

FOLLOW-UP

CONTACT NUMBER	FOLLOW-UP COMMENTS	PERSON SPOKEN TO	SCHEDULED FOLLOW-UP DATE	ACTUAL FOLLOW UP DATE
1)				
2)				
3)				
4)				
5)				
6)				
7)				
8)				
9)				
10)				

NOTES

by phone is okay. A recommended follow-up process will be discussed in this chapter. A Follow-up Tracking Form has been provided for you (see figure 5.2). Complete one of these forms for each company in order to record every follow-up effort until mystery shopping assignments have been received.

STEP ONE

Compile/Maintain a Listing of Mystery Shopping Companies

As noted, the job of compiling a listing of mystery shopping companies has been taken care of for you. The listing of companies that appears in chapter 6 of this book includes companies that hire mystery shoppers located in large geographical areas. Some hire shoppers who reside in cities all over North America, and a few hire people residing in other countries as well. Companies that limit their work to local client firms and that, therefore, hire only locally based mystery shoppers are not included.

You may add to the list in this book by looking in your local phone book under the listing of "Shopper," "Shopping," "Shopping Services," or "Shoppers." Some of the companies listed will provide shopping services for those who cannot leave home because of illness or old age, for visitors from other countries, and/or for busy executives. Typically, these companies do not hire mystery shoppers. However, in many metropolitan areas, other companies advertising in the Yellow Pages section of local phone books provide mystery shopping services and contract with mystery shoppers to undertake assignments for them. By contacting these companies in addition to those listed in this book, you will have more potential firms to work with.

Remember that the more companies that offer you assignments, the more money you will be able to make from mystery shopping. In addition, when many companies are offering assignments to you, you will find yourself able to pick and choose assignments. You can select only those that are high paying or only those that are of the type that you like. Therefore, it makes sense to offer your services as a mystery shopper to as many mystery shopping companies as possible.

You should also consider working with companies that hire only experienced mystery shoppers. If you follow the steps outlined in this chapter, you should have your first mystery shopping assignment within a few days. After completing that assignment, you can honestly approach companies that hire only experienced mystery shoppers and truthfully tell them that you have experience. A current source of mystery shopping companies is *The Mystery Shopper*, a newsletter published four times a year that costs only $19.95 (U.S.) or $37 (Canadian) per year for those who read this book. Each issue features mystery shopping companies that hire experienced mystery shoppers. Companies that hire experienced shoppers tend to pay better than those that hire newcomers to the field. Most shoppers find that they earn back what they paid for the newsletter from their first mystery shopping assignment. By subscribing, a mystery shopper can continuously offer his or her services to more and more companies and maximize income generated from mystery shopping. To subscribe, fill out the Mystery Shopping Companies Experienced Shopper Newsletter

Subscription Form located at the end of this book, tear it out, and send it together with your check to the address listed on the form.

STEP TWO

Write: Asking for Assignments

Your initial contact with mystery shopping companies should be a letter expressing interest in working with them as a mystery shopper. The Sample Letter Requesting Employment (see figure 5.1) has proven to be effective. Many report that, after using this letter as a source for their own letters, they get forms back from mystery shopping companies by return mail and get assignments as soon as the forms are filled out and returned. But please do **not** use this form letter in spite of the fact that it has been exceedingly successful.

Asking you not to use this successful form letter may sound like a ludicrous request. Please keep in mind, however, that this is a form letter. All of the mystery shopping companies have received the same form letter many times before from those who have read this book. And that presents a problem. Judith Rappold, president of Business Resources–Mystery Shopping, in Austin, Texas, says that she likes to hire shoppers who have read this book. People who have the knowledge from this book, she notes, do a good job and are excellent mystery shoppers. However, Judith also stresses, she does **not** like to receive the form letter from this book. The reason is that although the form letter says the right things, it is a form letter—and she has received it many times. Judith stresses that mystery shoppers need to compose shopping reports, and she normally uses the letter of application from aspiring mystery shoppers to gauge their ability to compose. When she gets a form letter, of course, Judith has no knowledge of the applicant's ability to compose. She (and many other mystery shopping company executives) asks that you include the key elements of the form letter, but put them in your own words and work them into a letter that sells you on your background as well as the information you have gleaned from reading this book. Use synonyms for the key words in the form letter or use phrases that mean the same or essentially the same thing. And work these into a format that fits you, a format and a letter that **you** compose.

The form letter includes all the basics needed. In fact, in its first two sentences it:

1. Identifies your location.
2. Stresses that you are both "qualified" and "analytical."
3. Says you will provide "detailed" reports.

All three of these points are important to mystery shopping companies. It is suggested that the letter you compose include all three points, but that your letter include the points stated in your own words.

In past correspondence, some readers have stated that they are uncomfortable with writing that they are "qualified" and especially that they are "highly qualified" mystery shoppers when, in fact, they have yet to execute their first shopping assignment. These readers want to be honest in their letters of application sent to mystery shopping companies, and they see a contradiction in saying that they are highly qualified when they have no experience as a mystery shopper. Their honesty is applauded. However, keep in mind that this is the first book that has been published on the subject of how to be a mystery shopper. Most mystery shoppers learn from trial and error. Mystery shopping executives frequently agree that the person who has read this book has a better understanding of how to be a good and effective mystery shopper than most people who have several months of experience mystery shopping. In other words, after reading this book, **you are a highly qualified mystery shopper!**

Remember that the number one reason mystery shopping companies drop new mystery shoppers is that they either do not complete the shopping assignment on time or they fail to send in the shopping report on time. The third sentence of the form letter lets the company know that you can be counted on to not only complete the shopping assignment on time, but that you will submit the completed shopping report within forty-eight hours of completing the shopping assignment (the time frame most mystery shopping companies work within). Again, in your letter emphasize—in your own words—that you can be counted on to complete the assignment as well as the report on time.

Your letter to mystery shopping companies should include some of yourself and the points that are unique to you. Let the mystery shopping company executives know that you are special. Point out strengths in your background which may be of benefit to them. If you have worked in retail, stress that you know retail—and tell the reader about your retail background. If you have a bookkeeping or accounting background, let them know that you have experience working with figures. Whatever your strengths are, emphasize them.

STEP THREE

Complete the Forms

You may be surprised at how many forms and documents you will receive after mailing letters to mystery shopping companies. Remember, each company is different. Each one is likely to require a slightly different set of documentation. But most mystery shopping companies will not give you an assignment until all the documents that they require have been filled out and returned to them. Therefore, tackle the stack of paperwork as soon as it comes in. This may be tedious, but look at it this way—the sooner you get completed paperwork back to the companies, the sooner you will be earning money as a mystery shopper.

You will be evaluated on the quality of the application documents you submit. All documents should be prepared neatly, and returned without stains or excessive folds. It is probably better to avoid drinking coffee while completing the forms. Please make sure that you check each document to make sure you are not skipping a line or a block that calls for some information. Even when the data requested does not apply to you, it is far better to enter into the block, "N/A" or "Not Applicable," than it is to leave the block or line blank. Shopping executives are likely to reason that a person who left one or more lines blank on his or her forms will do the same thing on a shopping report. The next step to that reasoning is to not hire the applicant. Avoid losing the job before you get it. Fill in each block and each line on each form.

Although each company is different, documentation tends to be the same or similar. The following are some of the documents shopping companies may expect from you.

A COMPLETED APPLICATION FORM Most companies will send you a blank application form. They expect you to complete it and return it to them. The forms tend to be standard and, fortunately, short. Unless the company specifies differently, the application form should be typed. Keep in mind, however, that some companies will ask that application forms be completed by hand. There are sections on many shopping reports where parts of the form will be hand-printed. In some cases, the entire shopping report will be completed by hand. In such cases the mystery shopping company's executives will use the completed application form as a way of judging how clearly you print. Therefore, on this and any other document that calls for you to hand-print information, make certain that your letters are clear and easily readable.

Some people are concerned about requests for information that needs to be typed because they do not own a typewriter. It is not suggested that you buy a typewriter to complete the application forms or to fulfill your role of being a mystery shopper. However, the purchase of a used typewriter at a swap meet can often be quite inexpensive. If you do not have a typewriter or plan to purchase one, however, you have a couple of other choices. A good option is to use your library. Almost all libraries have typewriters that can be used by patrons at the library. Sometimes there is an hourly rental fee for using a library typewriter. If you are not sure whether or not your library has typewriters available to patrons, call first. If they do not have typewriters, ask the librarian where the closest library is that does have typewriters. A second choice is local colleges or universities. Many have keyboarding labs available for students and the general public to use. These labs are equipped with typewriters, word processors, and/or computers—any of which can work for you. Again, some will charge an hourly fee to use their equipment, but some make it available for limited amounts of time at no cost. Here, too, it is best to call before you go and let your dialing finger help you avoid needless walking.

Keep in mind that there is a third choice. This is to complete the form by hand. If you phone the shopping company and tell the executive that you do not own a typewriter, the shopping company executive will often agree to accept your application form (and any other document that their instruction sheet says should be typed) in clear, neat hand-printing.

A SHOPPER PROFILE FORM Glance at the sample shopper profile form (see figure 5.3, Shopper Profile Form). The profile is a document the shopping companies use to determine the kind of shopper that you are. The mystery shopping company executive who receives your documents will want to know what types of things you shop for on a regular basis. As you can see, the profile asks if you shop for food; women's, infants', children's, and/or men's clothing; over-the-counter medicines; and so forth. Be honest. More than one mystery shopping company owner has indicated that he or she will never hire a person who checks the "yes" block on each item and/or states that they buy large quantities in each of the shopping categories listed on the profile. Checking each block "yes" or indicating that you buy a lot of each type of item suggests to them that the shopper applicant is either lying or not paying attention to the questions asked.

It is suggested that you follow the 10 percent rule. Look at each line of the profile. Identify one item out of every ten types of shops (things you are asked if you buy in quantity) and answer "no" or indicate that you buy little or none of that product or service. It is beneficial to say "no" to at least one in ten areas of shopping even if you, in fact, do buy a lot of each item listed.

Either at the end or at the beginning of most profiles are lines to indicate any other types of shopping you do. A person who buys many airline tickets, for example, might enter the words, "Travel agency" here. A person who is heavily into amateur photography might enter, "Photo processing" here. Try to always list some type of shopping which you do and which is not represented on the preprinted check-off lines. This will show the mystery shopping company reader that you have given thought to the profile and that it is not just another form to you.

AN INDEPENDENT CONTRACTOR FORM Mystery shopping companies have the choice of hiring you as an employee or contracting with you as an independent contractor. Almost all consider mystery shoppers to be independent contractors. If they do so, they must

Figure 5.3 Shopper Profile Form

SHOPPER PROFILE FORM

INFORMATION: In making mystery shopping assignments, we strive to match the shopping experience of our shoppers with the needs of our clients. For example, if we contract to provide shops for a baby products retail chain, we attempt to offer these assignments to our shoppers who are mothers and who for many years have been buying baby clothing and other baby products. Experienced mothers tend to have a wider knowledge of the market, ask more appropriate questions, and be accepted as "normal" shoppers much more rapidly than would other shoppers (a single male in his forties, for example). It is for this reason, therefore, that we ask for your shopping profile. We will make every effort to provide you with assignments that fit or match your profile.

INSTRUCTIONS: Please print or type your name and other information requested. Then, read every entry and check the block at the right which best describes your shopping pattern as it relates to the type of buying described. On the "Other" lines at the bottom, please enter any other type of shopping you do.

Your Name: ____________________

Your Address (including zip): ____________________

Your Shopper Number for our company (if one has been assigned): ____________

DO YOU BUY?	YES	NO	VERY MUCH	A LOT	SOME	VERY LITTLE	NEVER
1) Groceries	( )	( )	( )	( )	( )	( )	( )
2) Sports Equipment	( )	( )	( )	( )	( )	( )	( )
Which Sport(s)							
3) Pet Food	( )	( )	( )	( )	( )	( )	( )
4) Pet Supplies	( )	( )	( )	( )	( )	( )	( )
5) Clothing							
Men's	( )	( )	( )	( )	( )	( )	( )
Women's	( )	( )	( )	( )	( )	( )	( )
Children's	( )	( )	( )	( )	( )	( )	( )
Infants'	( )	( )	( )	( )	( )	( )	( )
Formal (Tux, Evening Gowns, etc.)	( )	( )	( )	( )	( )	( )	( )
6) Hardware	( )	( )	( )	( )	( )	( )	( )
7) Small Appliances	( )	( )	( )	( )	( )	( )	( )
8) Large Appliances	( )	( )	( )	( )	( )	( )	( )
9) Household Repair Supplies and Equipment	( )	( )	( )	( )	( )	( )	( )
10) Jewelry							
Men's	( )	( )	( )	( )	( )	( )	( )
Women's	( )	( )	( )	( )	( )	( )	( )
11) Other (What?)	( )	( )	( )	( )	( )	( )	( )
12) Other (What?)	( )	( )	( )	( )	( )	( )	( )

have an independent contractor form signed by you before they may legally pay you. Therefore, when you receive an independent contractor form in the mail, sign and date it, fill in your name (printed) and enter your Social Security number in the appropriate blocks. Then return the completed form to the mystery shopping company. Those four blocks (1. name printed, 2. name signed, 3. Social Security number, and 4. date) are the only ones on the form, so it is one of the easiest forms to complete. If you do not complete the form and return it, you may wind up doing the work and not getting paid for it. Keep in mind, however, that most mystery shopping companies simply will not give assignments to a mystery shopper until they have a signed independent contractor form on file for the shopper.

A BLANK CUSTOMER SERVICE EVALUATION FORM This is a form that goes by many names. It is the most important of all forms from the point of view of most mystery shopping companies, and it has many titles. It is the form that is completed at the end of a shopping assignment by the mystery shopper evaluating how well the employees of the firm did their job and evaluating the shopping environment (cleanliness of store and restroom, neatness of displays of goods, and so forth). The form is most often referred to simply as a shopping report, but its official name is usually something like "Customer Service Evaluation Form."

Take a minute to review the completed mystery shopping report form sample at the beginning of chapter 3 (see figure 3.2, Example of a Shopping Report). Some mystery shopping company executives want to get a feel for how well a potential mystery shopper can fill out a shopping report. They will send you a blank form and ask that you shop for something you would normally buy anyway. After purchasing the item, they ask that you complete their blank customer service evaluation form (shopping report) based on your shopping experience while purchasing the item. They will not pay you for this, and they will not reimburse you for your expenses. After all, their instructions are that you should buy something you would normally buy anyway. When they receive your completed report, it will be evaluated. They will ask the following questions:

1. How detail-oriented were you?
2. Were you able to get answers to all the questions on their form?
3. Did you report both the positives and the negatives of the shopping experience?
4. How well did you pick up on small points?

When you submit the completed report, make sure that it is typed and feel free to add information that you think will make the report better when you get to the end of the evaluation form.

YOUR RÉSUMÉ A few companies will ask you to send them your résumé. If you have a current résumé, send them the one that you have. If not, don't worry. Even if you have not prepared a résumé for many years, it need not be a difficult task. Go to your library and check out two or three books on writing résumés. What most mystery shopping companies want is a short, one-page résumé. Start with your name, address, and contact phone number in the top center of the page. Make sure the phone number is one that is connected to an answering machine, in case you are gone when the mystery shopping company representative calls you with an assignment. Skip a couple of lines and center your first heading, "Experience," in the middle of the page. If you have experience in retail, accounting, finance, or customer service, list these jobs first under a subheading of, "Related Experience." If not, start with a subheading of, "Shopping Experience." Briefly identify areas where you consider yourself an "expert" shopper. Finally, under a subheading of, "Other Experience," list any other experience or work history that you feel will be appropriate.

The next major section will start with the term, "Education," centered in the middle of the page. Under this start by putting in the fact that you have read this book. The entry might look like this:

> *The Mystery Shopper*, a book by J. Poynter,
> was read and thoroughly digested.

Under the "Education" section, you should add any degrees you have received and the institutions awarding those degrees. Some companies look for a cross section of shoppers, and knowing what your highest attained educational level is will help them place you in one of the appropriate segments of their cross sections.

The final part of your résumé should be headed with the title, "Other," centered in the middle of the page. This is the place where you may include any other data that will help to sell you. If you did voluntary work that involved quality control, list it. That experience will tell the mystery shopping company that you have some type of background in quality control. If you were the treasurer of a club, association, or organization, include a reference to that effect. This will show the company that you understand finance and financial transactions. In other words, put anything else here that will help encourage the mystery shopping company executives to want to give you assignments as a mystery shopper.

STEP FOUR

Follow-up

Keeping in mind that the goal is to work for as many mystery shopping companies as possible, follow-up is frequently absolutely essential. Many companies will respond right away, sending you their forms and documents to be completed and returned. From other companies, you may hear nothing. Keep in mind that generally speaking the companies that pay the best are those whose headquarters are located the furthest away from you. However, it is the policy of some of these companies to not contact a mystery shopper applicant until assignments in his or her area are open. For some companies, assignments in your area will be rare. Also keep in mind that mystery shopping companies give first priority in making assignments to experienced mystery shoppers who have successfully completed shopping assignments with their company in the past. The second priority will be experienced mystery shoppers who have worked with other companies, but may be new with them. As a new mystery shopper (a person who has not conducted shops for any company in the past), you will fall into their last or third priority. However, do not despair. Company executives know that those people who express a strong interest in working with them will ultimately be their best mystery shoppers. Therefore, it is necessary to walk that fine line between contacting companies frequently enough to let them know that you have a strong interest in working with them and contacting them so frequently that they think you are "bugging" them.

Generally speaking, it is appropriate to send a follow-up letter to companies every six weeks. If the company has a phone number listed, alternate follow-up letters with follow-up phone calls. In other words, start with a letter. Six weeks later, place a phone call to the company and tell the executive with whom you speak that you have written to the company and that you are especially interested in receiving a mystery shopping assignment from them. Six weeks later, send a nice follow-up letter indicating that you are still interested in working with them. Continue alternating between letters and phone calls until either you receive a first assignment or you are given some indication that you will never get work with the company. If there is no phone number, you will need to rely on letters. Do so. Send out a nice reminder letter every six weeks.

Keep in mind that your follow-up needs to be conducted with each company on the list in this book. However, follow-ups will also be needed with companies you have found by yourself through your local phone book and with companies listed in each issue of *The Mystery Shopper* if you have elected to subscribe to that newsletter.

Make photocopies of the follow-up tracking form (see figure 5.2). It is suggested that you ask the person who makes photocopies for you to copy the follow-up tracking form onto "card" stock. It will be a little more expensive than copying on standard paper, but card stock is sturdier and some of your tracking form sheets will receive a lot of handling. Fill out one tracking form for each company and keep all your forms in a "tickler" file, i.e., a date-oriented file. Each time you make a phone call or send a letter note it on the tracking form. If it was a phone call, indicate what the person at the mystery shopping company said and make a note as to what you should do. For example, if the person you spoke with said the company has nothing in your area at this time, but expects to get a contract requiring shopping in your area in about three months, put a note on the tracking form to that effect and put a follow-up date two-and-a-half months later on the form. Then drop the form in the file for the day or week two-and-a-half months later when you plan to follow up. If you sent a letter, note the date of the letter on the tracking form, enter the date of your next follow-up (six weeks later) on the tracking form, attach a copy of the letter to the form, and put the form into your tickler file for the day or week when you will next follow up (six weeks later). Be sure to check your tickler file every day or at least every week so that your follow-ups will be carried out in a timely manner.

After you start getting assignments, you may want to divide your tracking files into two groups—those companies with which you have undertaken one or more assignments (these are your "Previously Worked" files) and those from which you have not yet received any assignments (these are your "Never Worked" files). Note the dates on which you receive each assignment on the tracking files of each company that has given you an assignment. Divide your "Previously Worked" files into "Active" and "Inactive." Active files will be those companies with which you have worked during the previous ninety days. Inactive files will be those companies that have not given you an assignment for ninety days. Go through your files at least once a month placing the tracking forms for previously worked companies into active and inactive files. Treat your inactive companies in the same way as you treat the companies that have not yet given you an assignment. In other words, start phoning and writing these companies every six weeks until they again become active by giving you another assignment. If you conscientiously work this tracking system, you will find that your receipt of assignments as a mystery shopper will grow faster and faster.

CHAPTER 6

NORTH AMERICA'S MYSTERY SHOPPING COMPANIES

Listing Criteria

Many companies have been included in the list of North America's mystery shopping companies, which constitutes the bulk of this chapter. However, many more companies have been excluded from the list. Several criteria were used. Primary was that the companies included had to be willing to hire someone without mystery shopping experience. In each case, we checked with company executives to make certain that the company does provide assignments to those who are brand new to mystery shopping. Most companies also hire people who are experienced mystery shoppers as well, but there were a few companies whose executives said that they far prefer to have people who are new to shopping.

A second criterion was geographical. Surveys of mystery shopping companies suggest that most are local, city-wide, or at most multicounty in their geographical coverage. These companies were not included since they tend to pay less money to mystery shoppers and they would not employ the vast majority of the readers of this book—people who are located throughout North America. We especially wanted to include companies with either a national or an international (United States and Canada) coverage. However, because there are so few of these, we also included companies that are regional. In each case, the company hires shoppers in three or more states, provinces, and/or territories. In most cases, however, their coverage is far greater than three states, provinces, and/or territories.

Some mystery shopping companies specialize. We attempted to include some companies in each of the major areas of specialization in the industry. However, companies that take on all types of work and are considered "Generalist" companies have been included as well.

List Dating

Mystery shopping companies, like all other companies, come and go. New ones are started every week, and some of the old ones disappear from time to time (sometimes it seems like every month). The list provided here is current as of the final proofing of this book. However, there are bound to be companies that will go out of business while this edition is in use. One should always update lists.

It is because of the issue of list dating that this book is published as a "short run," i.e., fewer copies are printed per edition than are prepared for many books.

New editions come out every two years. This, of course, substantially increases the cost per book. However, by preparing a new edition every two years, we are able to make certain that the list is kept as current as possible (for a book). It also means that the book you have purchased will have fairly up-to-date information on companies in it. If there are any books from a previous edition that have not been sold when a new edition comes out, they are thrown away. The author wants to make absolutely certain that the information on companies, which you receive, is as current and accurate as possible.

But even more frequent updates are beneficial. It is suggested that you subscribe to *The Mystery Shopper*, a newsletter for mystery shoppers. Each issue not only identifies address/phone number changes and companies that have changed some key aspect of their business structure, but each issue also identifies mystery shopping companies that have not previously been featured either in this book or in a previous issue of the newsletter. In most cases, these are not "new" mystery shopping companies. Rather, they are companies that because of an expansion of their activities are now firms that we think our subscribers would benefit from working with. An application form for a subscription to *The Mystery Shopper* appears at the back of this book.

Six Kinds of Information

The companies listed in this chapter are presented in alphabetical order. In each case, the contact information which company executives themselves want to have listed is listed. For each listing, there are two sections:

a top section and a bottom section. Six kinds of information appear for most companies listed. Contact information is at the top. The other five kinds of information are included in the bottom section. These are:

1. Areas of specialization.
2. Geographical coverage information.
3. Application method preference.
4. Compensation.
5. Distinctive ways of operation or shopper expectations.

In the top part of each listing, the information provided normally includes the name of the company, the mailing address (unless company executives only want shopper applicants to apply online and, therefore, do not want their address listed), an e-mail address and/or home page address (if company executives want this information listed), and a phone number (unless company executives have asked us to leave it out because they do not want shopper applicants calling their offices).

The lower part of the listing tells something about the company. In a few cases, these descriptors have been totally written by a company executive (usually the president of the company). In such cases, the information is limited to that which the company executive wants to appear.

SPECIALIZATIONS In most cases, the lower part of the listing will include a discussion of any shopping areas in which the company specializes. Some companies only offer one type (one specialization) of shopping. Others offer a wide variety of types of shopping (specializations), and still other companies provide any type of shopping that a client company may ask for. Generally, the shopping "types," "specializations," or "categories" will be one or more of the following: Automotive, Banking/Financial, Food and Beverage (everything from fast food to fine dining), Gas Station/Convenience Store, Grocery Shopping, Home/Apartment (real estate), Lodging (hotels, motels, and/or resorts), Retail (department stores and specialty stores), and Telephone (shopping assignments that are completed on the phone).

GEOGRAPHICAL COVERAGE If company executives are willing to provide it, the lower part of the listing will include geographical coverage information. This edition of the book is sold in the United States and Canada. Therefore, the geographical coverage information is limited to those two countries, i.e., North America. Many of the mystery shopping companies listed have shopping assignments throughout North America—in all major and in many smaller cities and towns throughout the United States and Canada. Other companies limit their coverage to just the United States or, with two or three companies, just to Canada. Some firms only operate in a few states, provinces, or territories. With each company, an effort has been made to identify what the geographic boundaries of operation are and to discuss them. Obviously, if you live in Toronto, you will not get an assignment from a company that limits its shopping opportunities to Florida, Georgia, and three or four other states in the southeastern part of the United States.

APPLICATION METHOD The third major piece of information provided in the lower part of each listing is how the company wants shopper applicants to apply with them. Many will want a letter addressed to the address provided. In fact, this should be considered the "default" option. In other words, if nothing is said about how to apply, writing a letter requesting application materials will be the best approach. In some cases, however, a mystery shopping company may want applicants to send them an e-mail or a fax. Still other companies will want applicants to pull up information about the company on the firm's home page. In such cases, an application form will be somewhere on the home page, and the mystery shopping company will want shopper applicants to fill out the application form (and other documents) online and send the completed forms back to the mystery shopping company online. Still other companies will give you a choice of how to apply.

COMPENSATION Compensation information is requested from mystery shopping companies. However, most companies will not provide specific compensation data. This book provides information that becomes "public knowledge." Many mystery shopping executives purchase a copy of each edition right after the book comes off the press. Because most mystery shopping executives are hesitant to share compensation information with their competitors, you will usually find either no information about compensation or the information provided will be quite general.

WAYS OF OPERATION AND SHOPPER EXPECTATIONS
Some mystery shopping companies have distinctive ways of operating or distinctive expectations from mystery shoppers. In the lower part of the listing, an effort has been made to discuss these corporate ways/ expectations wherever it is believed that the knowledge of these will benefit shopper applicants.

A Selected Listing of Better Mystery Shopping Companies That Hire New Mystery Shoppers

A CLOSER LOOK

Post Office Box 920760
Norcross, Georgia 30010
E-mail: info@closer-look.com
Web site: www.a-closer-look.com

Since 1994 A Closer Look (ACL) has provided the hotel and restaurant industry with excellent shopping feedback as well as the best shoppers in the business. Shoppers are sought throughout the United States and Canada. Applicants must have the ability to make keen observations and transfer these observations to a well-written and grammatically correct format. Those who want to shop with the firm need to access the following home page: www.a-closer-look.com and follow the online directions.

AUDITS & SURVEYS WORLDWIDE (CYBERSHOPPERS)

650 Avenue of the Americas
New York City, New York 10011
E-mail: mshoppers@surveys.com
Web site: cybershoppers.surveys.com

Cybershoppers is a division of Audits and Surveys Worldwide. The firm specializes in competitive shopping, department store and specialty shops, and new car shops. Compensation ranges from $12 to $90, and shopping assignments are throughout the United States and Canada. Executives at Cybershoppers ask that applicants apply online at http://cybershoppers.surveys.com.

BARE ASSOCIATES INTERNATIONAL

3251 Old Lee Highway, Suite 209
Fairfax, Virginia 22030
Web site: www.baiservices.com

Bare Associates International Inc., a worldwide shopping company based in Northern Virginia and Antwerp, Belgium, hires shoppers worldwide on an as-needed basis. Clients include hospitality accounts, retail, golf courses, groceries, airports, and health clubs to name just a few. It prefers to hire experienced mystery shoppers, but will consider individuals without experience if they meet other criteria. Shoppers must have flexibility in scheduling and the ability to fax reports and to receive and send e-mail. Fees and reimbursement are paid for some types of shops; reimbursement only for others.

BEYOND HELLO, INC.

Post Office Box 5240
Madison, Wisconsin 53705-0240
Web site: www.beyondhello.com

Shoppers are needed throughout the United States, Canada, Puerto Rico, and Guam. The firm started in the factory outlet industry, and it still has client stores in many outlets. Although a wide variety of retailers are clients, the biggest single client base is full-service shoe stores. A range of compensations is paid, and there are some assignments that require the shopper to return the item purchased. A strong emphasis is on politeness. Please register online by visiting www.BeyondHello.Com. This will enable Beyond Hello to consider you for future assignments.

BUSINESS EVALUATION SERVICES

2920 "F" Street, Suite E-15
Bakersfield, California 93301
Phone: (888) 300-8292
Web site: www.mysteryshopperservices.com

Business Evaluation Services is a full service mystery shopping company. It services clients nationwide and performs evaluations for a wide variety of industries. It provides online reporting for both shoppers and clients. Work is easy to find with this company, as it has its own online job posting board. After you have become a registered shopper with Business Evaluation Services, you can log in and view available assignments by state and city. This makes locating shops simple. Also, you can automatically apply for any assignment that you are interested in conducting.

If you are not already registered with Business Evaluation Services, you can do so at www.mysteryshopperservices.com by logging on at the services for mystery shoppers' section and selecting the registration page. If you do not have Web access, you can call and request a fax registration form as an alternative.

BUSINESS RESOURCES–MYSTERY SHOPPING

2222 Western Trails Boulevard, #107
Austin, Texas 78745
Phone: (512) 416-7702

Judith Rappold is the president of Business Resources–Mystery Shopping. The firm has assignments throughout the United States and Canada. The largest contracts are in the Southwest, particularly Texas. Application letters are often used as indications of the person's professionalism and ability to compose reports. The company is less likely to call someone who has used a "form" letter when requesting employment. To apply with Business Resources, send a professional résumé and a letter indicating what geographical areas you will accept work in.

BYERS CHOICE INC.

Web site: www.byerschoiceinc.com

Many shoppers say that Byers Choice pays shoppers more rapidly than any other company. In fact, in talking with the owner of Byers Choice, Bob Petit, he noted that checks had been written and sent out for reports received that same morning. Shoppers are sought for assignments throughout the United States, and assignments include convenience stores, fast food, some competitive shopping, and miscellaneous other assignments. Shoppers must have a car and Internet access. Apply online at the Web site noted above.

CERTIFIED REPORTS, INC.

Post Office Box 447
7 Hudson Street
Kinderhook, New York 12106

Recruiting throughout the United States and Canada, Certified Reports has merchandising and mystery shopping assignments in all of the fifty states and Canada. The preferred way of applying is by calling the company's toll-free number, 1-800-320-1290. It is important to listen carefully to the directory and the instructions. Applicants will need to speak to the appropriate "zone manager." The zone manager for your area will inform you of any assignments in your area. Application materials will be mailed to you shortly after your discussion with the zone manager. Please complete all application materials and return them to the attention of the appropriate zone manager at the above address.

CONSUMER IMPRESSIONS, INC.

1601 Dorchester, Suite 107
Plano, Texas 75075

Consumer Impressions offers client companies a multitude of ways to evaluate the "impressions" their consumers take away from a visit to their places of business. Mystery shopping is one of these ways. The firm actively seeks shoppers who report their "impression" of the entire shopping experience, not just an evaluation of how the sales person handled the transaction. Shoppers are hired throughout the United States. Applicants should write a letter requesting employment as local mystery shoppers. Letters should be sent to the address above.

COURTESY COUNTS, INC.

7825 Tuckerman Lane, Suite 213
Potomac, Maryland 29854
E-mail: www.courtesycounts.com

Courtesy Counts provides retail and point-of-sale store audits throughout the United States. It has been in business for twenty-two years and hires shoppers on an as-needed basis throughout the country. Apply online by using the above e-mail address.

CUSTOMER PERSPECTIVES

213 West River Road
Hooksett, New Hampshire 03106-2628
E-mail: recruiter@customerperspectives.com
Web site: www.customerperspectives.com

Customer Perspectives is a nationwide firm with an emphasis on top-notch quality. It has been in business for more than eighteen years. Shoppers are hired from throughout the United States. Assignments may include competitive shopping, department store and specialty shops, banks, grocery store shops, hotel and other lodging, or real estate shops. In addition, you might be asked to shop for gasoline, food, or a new car. Shoppers must meet specifications and deadlines of both the client and of Customer Perspectives. Also they must have Internet and e-mail access and submit a writing sample. In addition to compensation for writing reports, Customer Perspectives reimburses the actual amount of purchases, required toll fees, and parking expenses. You may apply in three ways. The preferred way is to access the following home page: www.customerperspectives.com. An alternative is to send an e-mail to: recruiter@customerperspectives.com. The third alternative is to send a letter addressed to "Recruiter" to the address noted above.

CUSTOMER'S VIEW, INC.

920 Country Club Drive, Suite 2B
Moraga, California 94556
Fax Number: 1-800-593-2629
E-mail: shoppers@customersview.com
Web site: www.CustomersView.com

Customer's View, Inc. offers assignments throughout the United States for gasoline purchases, food and beverage shopping, grocery store shops, movie theater shops, and competitive shopping. The company is looking for detail-oriented shoppers with the ability to write clearly. Shoppers must also have Internet and e-mail access and the ability to receive e-mail messages. In addition, shoppers must be able to fax and scan documents. Customer's View, Inc. has been in business for more than five years. The firm is moving toward an online system where its shoppers and clients can access and submit information via the company's Web site. To apply, access the following home page: www.customersview.com

EVALUATION SYSTEMS FOR PERSONNEL

2990 Richmond Avenue, Suite 650
Houston, Texas 77098
Fax: (713) 528-3710
E-mail: ESPShop@ESPSHOP.Com
Web site: www.espshop.com

Started in 1987, Evaluation Systems for Personnel hires shoppers in cities throughout North America. Shopping assignments may include banking, private storage, hospitals, hardware stores, furniture stores, health clubs, and cruise line shops. Applicants may apply in three ways, but in each case the contact should be Jennifer Tran, senior coordinator. You may send a letter, send an e-mail, or access the company's home page. The above listing provides the contact information for each option. Compensation varies, but the company has an excellent reputation for paying shoppers on time.

FEEDBACK PLUS, INC.

5580 Peterson Lane, Suite 120
Dallas, Texas 75240-5157
Web site: www.gofeedback.com

Feedback Plus, Inc. employs more than 100,000 shoppers with assignments throughout the United States and Canada. Specialties include retail stores, restaurants, and financial services. Shoppers must have an e-mail address and access to the Internet. Apply using the Internet address noted above. The interviewed company executive stressed that the only way to apply is through the Web site.

GAME FILM CONSULTANTS

6300 Richmond, Suite 208
Houston, Texas 77057

This firm hires new shoppers, and it employs shoppers throughout the United States. Quality control is emphasized, and shoppers are required to wear both a microphone (to tape conversations) and a tiny video camera (to photograph conversations). Game Film Consultants trains all its shoppers to be qualified and comfortable for each shopping experience. There are a wide variety of assignments, and many assignments are in a retail environment and/or setting. Write to Game Film Consultants at the address above.

GREEN AND ASSOCIATES

Web site: www.greenandassociates.com

Green and Associates specializes in food and beverage establishments, including some of the better upscale chains. In addition, shoppers may also receive assignments to shop for other (non-food) retailers as well as hotel shopping assignments. The firm hires shoppers in thirty-two states of the United States and in most of the Canadian provinces and territories. It has a few assignments in other countries, as well. Green and Associates prefers to hire shoppers who have a college degree, and it insists on shoppers having good communication skills. Shoppers must have Internet access, and it is best if you own your own computer system with Internet capability. Applications are only taken by computer.

Pull up the Green and Associates home page by entering: www.greenandassociates.com.

INFOTEL

3190 South Bascom Avenue, Suite 100
San Jose, California 95124
Web site: www.infoteljobboard.com

Infotel has one of the biggest client representation lists of any mystery shopping company. It represents companies in cities and towns all over North America, including Disney Stores, the Banana Republic, and Brooks Brothers. You can either send a letter requesting an application (to the address above) or you can apply online at www.infoteljobboard.com. This company currently requires that its shoppers have Internet access and current e-mail. In either case, having a completed application on file is required before assignments will be provided.

INNOVATIVE MARKETING INCORPORATED

40 Eglinton Avenue East, Suite 701
Toronto, Ontario
Canada M4P 3A2

I.M.I. is a marketing research company located in the Toronto, Ontario, Canada area. Although the primary job of I.M.I. is conducting telephone and mail surveys, the company has an ongoing mystery shopping program service with hotel and retail chains. Now and then I.M.I. contracts for other mystery shopping, which is why the firm always needs shoppers. At the present time, I.M.I. is of a medium size, but the company is growing fast. Types of mystery shopping that the company has contracted for in the past has been getting shoppers to open up a bank account and write up a report on it, calling a beer company and requesting an information packet, and going to malls to note traffic flow. I.M.I. has also done retail shops to verify product placement and the presence of signage. For those wishing to become mystery shoppers with I.M.I., a letter should be written to: Michael Crossett, Mystery Shop Program, I.M.I., 40 Eglinton Avenue E., Suite 701, Toronto, Ontario, M4P 3A2 Canada.

MARKETING SYSTEMS UNLIMITED, CORP.

E-mail: info@msultd.com
Web site: www.msultd.com

Marketing Systems Unlimited Corporation offers full-time employment to independent contractors in forty-six states of the United States. Shopping assignments are gas stations, convenience stores, fast food shopping, and a few lodging establishments. Shoppers will have some expenses, such as transportation by car, but a large number of assignments are provided. Compensation ranges from $10 to $40 per assignment. Apply by sending an e-mail message to info@msultd.com, attention HRM, requesting an application for employment.

MARKET VIEWPOINT

995 Fairview Road, Suite 202
Glenmoore, Pennsylvania 19343-1813
Fax: (610) 942-7031
E-mail: info@marketviewpoint.com
Web site: www.marketviewpoint.com

The clients of Market Viewpoint are quite varied. All of the traditional types of companies are represented. However, concentration is on service business operations. Shopper compensation ranges from $10 for a quick in/out type of shop to $50 for a far more involved shop (and a much more detailed shopping report). Shopping assignments are throughout the United States. There is, as yet, nothing in Canada. To apply to work with the company as a shopper, you may send a letter, fax, or e-mail to the president of Market Viewpoint, Angela V. Megasko, using the contract information above. However, shoppers are encouraged to apply online with Market Viewpoint at: www.marketviewpoint.com

MICHELSON & ASSOCIATES, INC.

1900 The Exchange, Suite 360
Atlanta, Georgia 20339
Web site: www.michelson.com/research

Michelson & Associates, Inc. is one of the largest mystery shopping companies and hires shoppers throughout North America.

The firm prefers to hire experienced shoppers, but often it has hired people who are new to mystery shopping. Applications are accepted by computer only. Go to the company's Web site (www.michelson.com/research). Access the new applicant information. Fill out the application form and send it back to the company via computer.

NATIONAL SHOPPING SERVICE NETWORK, LLC.

3910 East Evans Avenue
Denver, Colorado 80210
Phone or Fax: (303) 451-0325
E-mail: howard@mysteryshopper.net
Web site: www.mysteryshopper.net

This innovative mystery shopping organization is blazing new trails in cyberspace. Mystery shoppers need only to log onto the Internet and access the screen where one applies to be a mystery shopper (www.mysteryshopper.net). During any month, there are mystery shopping assignments in the United States, Canada, and the United Kingdom. NSSN's corps of Internet-savvy shoppers then file their reports online. If you run into problems with the process, leave an e-mail message with Howard Troxel at the e-mail address above. He is one of the organization's founders.

QUALITY ASSESSMENTS MYSTERY SHOPPERS

Post Office Box 90547
Austin, Texas 78709
Web site: www.QAMS.com

The bulk of the assignments with Quality Assessments Mystery Shoppers are in the southern and western parts of the United States, but this fifteen-year-old company hires shoppers for work all over the United States (nothing in Canada yet). The firm specializes in retail businesses and restaurants, but it has some other types of assignments as well. To apply for work with Quality Assessments Mystery Shoppers, go to its Web site at www.qams.com. Click on "Shopper Resources" on the link on the left side of the Web page. Carefully read the instructions, and then fill out the online shopper information form.

J. M. RIDGWAY

1066 Saratoga Avenue, Suite 120
San Jose, California 95129-3401
Web site: www.jmridgway.com

This national firm prefers, but does not limit itself to, experienced shoppers. For fastest employment, apply online at its Web site: www.jmridgway.com. It is okay to mail your résumé if you have no access to Internet, but e-mail/techno shoppers will get the majority of the work. Do not call.

S.G. MARKETING GROUP, INC.

Post Office Box 773
Arnold, California 95223
Phone: 1-888-313-7464
Fax: 1-888-511-7467
E-mail: sgm@sgmarketing.com
Web site: www.sgmarketing.com

Specializing in sales and service evaluations of financial institutions and retail stores, the S.G. Marketing Group is quite demanding of high quality work. Nevertheless, executives of the firm point out, conducting shops for the firm is fun, challenging, and rewarding. Many of the shops conducted for the S.G. Marketing Group relate to bank shops. Shoppers pose as new customers opening accounts or requesting loans. Concerns relate to how well and how polite bank employees are when handling these transactions. Compliance is also a strong issue, and some shops will emphasize how well employees stayed in compliance with regulatory guidelines. Shoppers are sought throughout the United States and Canada. Access the company Web site for more information on specific locations and for an application form: www.sgmarketing.com.

SALES BUILDERS MARKETING, INC.

2206 East Magnolia
Phoenix, Arizona 85034
E-mail: brewer4@sbmarketing.com
Web site: www.sbmarketing.com

Food and beverage, department stores, and specialty shops are the specialties of Sales Builders Marketing, Inc. The firm has been in business since 1991 and offers clients a full range of options. These include mystery shopping, merchandising, in-store demos, and special events. Therefore shopper applicants may well find related work available in addition to mystery shopping. Midwestern and southern states west of Texas and including Texas are the areas where most shopping opportunities are found with this company. You may apply by mail, e-mail, or by accessing the company's home page. See the addresses above.

SERVICESENSE

Post Office Box 608JP
Norwell, Massachusetts 02061

Treating its mystery shoppers as well as it treats its customers is a source of pride for ServiceSense. The firm hires shoppers in twenty-two states, but the bulk of its assignments are for shops conducted in southern California and in the northeastern states of the United States. To apply, send a handwritten letter of interest to ServiceSense. Use the address noted above.

SERVICE EVALUATION CONCEPTS

55 East Ames Court
Plainview, New York 11803
Phone: 1-800-695-4746
E-mail: feedback@serviceevaluation.com
Web site: www.serviceevaluation.com

The executives of this firm are experts in the administrative process of mystery shopping. As a result, there are a wide variety of shopping assignments for those who work with them. Assignments are available in cities throughout the United States and Canada. Shoppers are considered business analysts. They must take a test on reading materials related to the policies and procedures of Service Evaluation Concepts. Those passing the test are given a password allowing them to go into the database and self-assign work. A business administrative rating is provided to shoppers determining the quality of work performed. It is on the basis of a shopper's business rating that better paid assignments are provided.

Applicants may apply online at the Web site or the e-mail address noted above or by mail by writing to the address above.

SERVICE PERFORMANCE GROUP, INC.

180 Detroit Street #B
Cary, Illinois 60013
Fax: (847) 516-9315
E-ail: www.serviceperformancegrp.com

Offering one of the largest shopping assignment ranges in the industry, Service Performance Group, Inc. shoppers may be assigned to undertake bank shops, competitive shopping, or dry cleaning and laundry shops. They may be asked to shop hotels or other lodging facilities, department stores, or specialty shops. Or they may shop for cell phones, a new car, or food at grocery stores. Assignments are throughout the United States and Canada. And the compensation for writing reports ranges from $10 to $125. Apply online at www.serviceperformancegrp.com

SERVICE QUEST

667 Boylston Street, Suite 200
Boston, Massachusetts 02116
E-mail: tturgeion@dataquestonline.com
Web site: www.dataquestonline.com

Service Quest is the mystery shopping division of Data Quest, a full-service, licensed corporate private investigations agency. The division specializes in both customer service and integrity quality assurance audits. Service Quest offers more than fifteen different types of shopping opportunities throughout the United States. While it prefers to hire experienced shoppers, it will consider hiring people who are new to mystery shopping. Compensation ranges from $10 to $200, and mileage is often reimbursed. Apply online at www.dataquestonline.com.

SER-VIEW

Two Carlson Parkway, Suite 350
Plymouth, Minnesota 55447
Fax: (763) 249-2478
E-mail: Ser-View@Ser-View.com
Web site: www.Ser-view.com

Health clubs, amusements, and attractions are a few of the more unusual types of assignments offered by Ser-View. In addition, the firm offers food and beverage, hotel and other lodging, department store and specialty shops, and competitive shopping assignments. Compensation ranges from nothing to $100 for writing shopping reports. The company seeks shoppers who are detail oriented, reliable, and able to communicate in a variety of contexts and individuals who provide timely reports. Internet access and e-mail ability are mandatory. Assignments are throughout the United States. Apply by sending an e-mail to the address above or at the firm's Web site (see above).

SHOPPERS' VIEW

4976 Plainfield Avenue, N.E.
Grand Rapids, Michigan 49525
Phone: (616) 445-0097
Web site: www.shoppersview.com

This firm provides work opportunities for shoppers throughout the United States and Canada. Specialties include retail, travel, banking, mortgage, rental/purchase, and food service. You may do competitive analyses or more traditional mystery shopping. Many shoppers are also offered opportunities to monitor customer satisfaction. To apply, register online. Use the Web site noted above.

SIGHTS ON SERVICE, INC.

Web site: www.secretshopper.com

Sights on Service, Inc. has been providing mystery shopping services to clients across America since 1990, and specializes in the hospitality and grocery industries. Secret Shopper is the registered trademark for its mystery shopping program. The company now provides Internet surveys and reports, in addition to the traditional methods of delivery. Shopper applications are taken only at its Web site (see above).

TESTSHOPPER.COM

10015 Old Columbia Road, Suite J-135
Columbia, Maryland 21046
Web site: www.testshopper.com

Testshopper.com specializes in transportation shops. The company owns and runs a major transportation company and knows the field well. Shopping assignments are located throughout the United States. Shoppers must have Internet access and must be able to file shopping reports online. Apply online by pulling up the home page and filling in the blanks. Then electronically transfer the completed application form to Testshopper.com.

THE GENESIS GROUP

1300 114th Avenue, S.E., Suite 220
Bellevue, Washington 98004
Phone: 1-425-688-8318
Web site: www.genesisgrp.com

Banks and retail are major clients of The Genesis Group. However, it also provides service for many other firms as well. Shoppers are sought throughout the United States. Mature shoppers with home-based computers and online access are sought. Shoppers must be able to transmit reports to the company within twenty-four hours of completing shops. Applicants should apply online using the Web site shown above.

THE LOCKSLEY GROUP

1011 Swarthmore Avenue
Pacific Palisades, California 90272
Phone: (310) 454-5105
Fax: (310) 454-0215
E-mail: LGLgroup@aol.com

The Locksley Group offers shopping opportunities throughout the United States and Canada. Compensation varies by assignment, but shopping specialties include specialty shops, food and beverage shopping, competitive shopping, department store shopping, and bank shops. The firm pays twice a month. You may apply by mail at the address above or by calling (310) 454-5105. You may also apply by e-mail to the following address: LGLGroup@aol.com

THE SECRET SHOPPER COMPANY

115 Olympic Place
Decater, Georgia 30030
Phone: (404) 377-8585
Toll-Free Phone: 1-877-770-8585
Fax: (404) 377-4780
E-mail: recruiters@secretshoppercompany.com
Web site: www.secretshoppercompany.com

The Secret Shopper Company is always seeking reliable individuals with excellent writing skills throughout the United States. The firm offers its shoppers a variety of assignments throughout the United States, Guam, Puerto Rico, and the Virgin Islands. Applicants are encouraged to visit its Web site (see above) and complete the Independent Contractor Agreement and the Shopper Application. As a result, your name will be in Secret Shopper's database. You will receive e-mail notifications when the company has assignments in your area. You will be able to log in using a specified username and password and view available assignments prior to accepting them (if notified). All of the reports for Secret Shopper are submitted online, so there is no worry about writing out reports and faxing them in. All reports are due twenty-four hours after completion of the assignment. Secret Shopper has a Skill Development Area on its Web site. It is a unique online training program for the industry and is beneficial for both new and experienced shoppers.

THE SHADOW AGENCY

1550 Norwood Drive, Suite 108
Hurst, Texas 76054
Phone: (817) 268-3338
Fax: (817) 280-9267
E-mail: shopper@theshaddowagency.com
Web site: www.theshadowagency.com

The Shadow Agency is the largest provider of video shopping in the United States. It does video, audio, written, and L.P. feedback shops. The range of assignments covers all mystery shopping areas of specialization. The pay ranges from $5 to $75, and shopping assignments are throughout the United States (including Hawaii and Alaska), Canada, Puerto Rico, and the Caribbean Islands. To apply, you may either send a message to the e-mail address noted above or access its Web site (also above). If you use the Web site, go to the "Employment" section.

TRENDSOURCE

111 Elm Street, Suite 100
San Diego, California 92101
Web site: www.trendsource.com

TrendSource has been in business for eleven years and engages shoppers throughout the United States and Canada. Shopping assignments are varied, but they include lodging, restaurant, clothing retailers, and grocery stores. Compensation varies, but frequently multiple assignments may be obtained. Apply on the company's Web site noted above.

WEBBTECH DATA SERVICES

Post Office Box 534
Huntington, New York 11743-0534
Web site: www.webbtech.com

Established in 1981 and with an extensive network of shoppers in two countries (the U.S. and Canada), WebbTech Data is one of the most experienced mystery shopping companies around. With twenty years in the industry, WebbTech Data has worked with all the top name firms in the retail, restaurant, gas station, and hotel industries. The company has worked on projects with multibillion-dollar manufacturers as well.

Although mystery shopping programs constitute WebbTech Data's "flagship" service, the company offers its clients several other data gathering programs as well. Therefore, shoppers with many different levels of experience are offered assignments. "The main issue above all," says WebbTech Data's president, "is to work with a reliable and detail-oriented shopper who follows directions. Since the proof is in the pudding, the majority of applicants get assignments." Often WebbTech Data Services will ask a shopper applicant to do a specified sample shop as part of the application process before "real" or "actual" assignments are offered. "With the high profile, major name clients we work with," WebbTech's president stressed, "WebbTech needs to know the caliber of the persons (shoppers) with whom we are working."

Applications are taken twenty-four hours a day, seven days a week by either e-mailing them to apply@webbtech.com or by logging on to www.webbtech.com and following the links to the "Shopper" section.

CHAPTER 7

WORKING WITH MULTIPLE MYSTERY SHOPPING COMPANIES

Expansion Options

If you are like most people, once you have started mystery shopping, you will love it. You will want to make it a way of life, and you will want to expand on your success. One of the nicest aspects about this field is that you can expand to whatever degree you wish. If you choose, mystery shopping can become a long-term part-time career to which you dedicate a substantial amount of your week (a job that takes twenty or more hours of your time each week). Or, if you prefer, you can own your own mystery shopping business. Or if you wish, you can become a full-time mystery shopper—conducting as many as ten shops per day five or six days a week and working with a large number of mystery shopping companies. Another option is to branch out into the multiple closely related industries that frequently draw upon the knowledge, skill, and background of experienced mystery shoppers. Alternatively, you may decide that you just want to do a few shops once in a while for fun and some good additional money. Essentially, whatever you want mystery shopping to be for you, the options are yours.

When newcomers to mystery shopping wish to expand beyond the shopping they have been doing for the mystery shopping companies that hire people who are new to mystery shopping, there are three directions the vast majority elect to take. Although most people choose to move in only one of the three directions, many choose two of the options and a few people work all three directions at the same time. The three options are:

TAKE ON BETTER-PAYING ASSIGNMENTS Many shoppers choose to expand their mystery shopping experiences and enhance their income from mystery shopping by working with the better-paying shopping assignments, and specializing in one or more of the better-paying types of mystery shopping. Because this is the most logical of the three specializations and because it is the direction most newcomers to the field take, it will be addressed first—in this chapter.

BECOME A MYSTERY SHOPPING BUSINESS OWNER Another direction mystery shoppers take to expand their income and opportunities is to become mystery shopping business owners. Typically, they start their own small, frequently specialized mystery shopping company. And, of course, the logical expansion from having a small, local, specialized company is to broaden it to a larger, regional (or national or international) company with multiple specializations. This direction will be explored in chapter 8.

BRANCH OUT INTO MULTIPLE RELATED INDUSTRIES Chapter 9 will round out the expansion chapters by addressing opportunities in related, closely associated fields. In chapter 9, we will explore each of these related fields and their relationship to mystery shopping.

Chapter 10, the final chapter in this book, will bring together all of the expansion opportunities by presenting a ten-step success process. By following this process, you are almost guaranteed to make a substantial amount of money from mystery shopping. Relatively few people elect to follow all ten steps, however, and that is okay. You may pick and choose. By following the success steps with which you are most comfortable, the probability is that you will rapidly attain the degree of success in mystery shopping that you envisioned when you first considered the possibility of becoming a mystery shopper. And not only will you be making a good income from mystery shopping, the probability is that you will be having a lot of fun with it as well.

Most Work for Only One Company

Most mystery shoppers start by working for one company, undertaking only one mystery shopping assignment at a time. You may become comfortable working for just one company and completing assignments as they come in. If so, soon you will become familiar with the way the company you work for wants its shops conducted and its reports filled out. Shopping for a familiar boss will become almost second nature. Many mystery shoppers—perhaps most—do just this. They work for one company and for only one company. However, by limiting yourself to work for a single company, you probably will also be limiting yourself to a limited income from mystery shopping.

Get Your First Assignment Right Away

Many people who read this book say to themselves that the system won't work. Or, they say that it may work for the aggressive, marketing-oriented person, but it won't work for them. However, the probability is that it **will work for you**. Getting a first assignment in a short period of time is the best way to get beyond this initial mental block. One of the best ways to do that is to contact the companies that will let you apply by computer. Although you should start by sending a letter of application to all companies in this book, where companies allow it, use your computer to make that first contact. The mail takes a day or two to go back and forth. Electronic communication can be instantaneous.

Computer-Based Mystery Shopping Companies

Several mystery shopping companies will take your application via computer on the Internet. Two of the first that do so are Michelson & Associates, Inc. and the National Shopping Service Network, LLC (NSSN). Generally speaking, if you have a computer and you are linked to the Internet, you may go to the Web sites of mystery shopping companies, find the mystery shopping application forms, fill in the forms, and transfer the completed forms back to the companies. It can all be done in a matter of a few minutes per company. Once the companies have the application data from you, they are in a position to start giving you shopping assignments.

Some who have read this book have obtained assignments the same day they read the book. After reading about applying via the Internet, they followed the procedures noted here, completed the application forms, electronically transferred the forms to the companies, and after as little as an hour (in one case), they received an assignment.

Of the two major companies, the best one to get an assignment from right away is NSSN. Although Michelson is a much larger company, many experienced shoppers already work for Michelson. It still gives assignments to newcomers every day because its assignment base is so large. However, because of its volume, some who are new have had to wait weeks for their first assignment from Michelson.

NSSN works a little differently than the standard Web site mystery shopping company approach discussed earlier. When you access the NSSN home page, you will be instructed to click on the "Employment Opportunities" option. When you get there, you should enter your name and other data about yourself. This will get your name on the NSSN Registry of mystery shoppers. The registry is free to you. Being in the NSSN Registry makes you eligible for potential NSSN assignments. When you are selected as a shopper, you will receive your shopping instructions by e-mail, and you will be able to file your shopping report online as well. From time to time, NSSN needs a large number of shoppers right away. Usually these assignments cover a wide geographical area (all of North America, all over the United States, or in several contiguous states or provinces). NSSN will send an e-mail message to all mystery shoppers in the registry who live in the targeted geographical area. The e-mail message will provide details of the assignment, and shoppers need only to send an e-mail back requesting an assignment in their area.

Bare Associates International also has a Web site, and the company encourages shoppers who want to work for the firm to take advantage of it. Market Viewpoint allows you to send a letter, fax, or e-mail, or apply online. Sales Builders allows you to apply by mail, e-mail, or at its Web site. The Locksley Group gives you three options: apply by mail, telephone, or e-mail.

Customer Perspectives and Evaluation Systems for Personnel offer slightly fewer options. With both companies, you may either apply by e-mail, at their Web site, or by writing them. Infotel allows you to either send a letter or to apply online. Service Evaluation Concepts, Ser-View, The Shadow Agency, and WebbTech Data Services let you apply by e-mail or at their respective Web sites.

Others that give you the opportunity to apply electronically include: A Closer Look, Audits & Surveys Worldwide (Cybershoppers), Beyond Hello, Business Evaluation Services, Byers Choice, Courtesy Counts, Customer's View, Feedback Plus, Inc., Green and Associates, Marketing Systems Unlimited, Quality

Assessments Mystery Shoppers, J.M. Ridgway, the S.G. Marketing Group, Service Performance Group, Service Quest, Shoppers' View, Sights on Service, Testshopper.com, The Genesis Group, The Secret Shopper Company, The Shadow Agency, and Trendsource.

Of course, applying with companies that allow you to apply using your home-based computer and the Internet is fine if you have a home-based computer linked to the Internet. However, if you do not, don't despair. In every major city, there is a cybercafé. This is a facility that normally serves food and Internet access. The charge for using the cybercafé's computers and accessing the Internet is usually between $15 and $25 per half hour; you probably won't need more than a half hour to access the shopping companies and fill out their application forms. To get a listing of cybercafés, buy (or check it out from your library) the one and only guidebook to cybercafés: *Cybercafés—A Worldwide Guide for Travelers* by Kath Stanton (ISBN 1890762016). As we go to press, the cost is $9.95 per copy. Get the second (or a later) edition (1997 publishing date).

To get assignments from the mystery shopping companies, you will need to have an e-mail address. You can get one assigned to you at no cost by applying at Yahoo.com (an Internet company and an Internet address). The computer address to contact for your private free e-mail address is: www.hotmail.com. Usually employees of the cybercafé will be happy to show you how to get the information you seek on the Internet and how to apply for your free e-mail address. (See figure 7.1.)

You may think all this work is too much effort in order to obtain shopping assignments from only a few

FIGURE 3.1 Mystery Shopping Companies' Web Sites

A Closer Look	www.a-closer-look.com
Audits & Surveys Worldwide (Cybershoppers)	cybershoppers.surveys.com
Bare Associates International	www.baiservices.com
Beyond Hello, Inc.	www.beyondhello.com
Business Evaluation Services	www.mysteryshopperservices.com
Byers Choice, Inc.	www.byerschoiceinc.com
Courtesy Counts	www.courtesycounts.com
Customer Perspectives	www.customerperspectives.com
Customer's View	www.CustomersView.com
Evaluation Systems for Personnel	www.ESPSHOP.COM
Feedback Plus, Inc.	www.gofeedback.com
Green and Associates	www.greenandassociates.com
Infotel	www.infoteljobboard.com
J.M. Ridgway	www.jmridgway.com
Market Viewpoint	www.marketviewpoint.com
Michelson & Associates, Inc.	www.michelson.com/research
National Shopping Service Network (NSSN)	www.mysteryshopper.net
Quality Assessments Mystery Shoppers	www.QAMS.com
S.G. Marketing Group, Inc.	www.sgmarketing.com
Sales Builders Marketing, Inc.	www.sbmarketing.com
Service Evaluation Concepts	www.serviceevaluation.com
Service Performance Group, Inc.	www.serviceperformancegrp.com
Service Quest	www.dataquestonline.com for
Ser-View	www.Ser-view.com
Shoppers' View	www.shoppersview.com
Sights on Service, Inc.	www.secretshopper.com
Testshopper.com	www.Testshopper.com
The Genesis Group	www.genesisgrp.com
The Secret Shopper Company	www.secretshoppercompany.com
The Shadow Agency	www.theshadowagency.com
Trendsource	www.trendsource.com
WebbTech Data Services	www.webbtech.com

companies. Most shoppers, however, say that it is less effort than writing a letter to each company. And, filling out the forms online is much faster than filling them out by hand or using a typewriter, even if you are a fast typist.

There is a similar process that can gain you assignments from several other mystery shopping companies that also use computers and their electronic mail capacity to provide work for mystery shoppers who wish to make their home-based computers help pay for themselves. Instead of accessing the companies' Web pages, however, you will be sending messages to mystery shopping company e-mail addresses. Again, get your own e-mail address (at a cybercafé or through your home-based Internet provider). Send a message to the e-mail address of every mystery shopping company that accepts e-mail applications. Fill out the application form that will be sent to you as an attachment to e-mail. Return the computer-generated application form via e-mail and wait for an assignment to be received by e-mail. Since everything is done electronically, you can apply for work and receive assignments while others are getting their letters of application in the mail. Many mystery shopping companies invite shoppers to apply for work electronically via e-mail (their e-mail addresses are provided in figure 7.2 and they are also listed in the company information data in chapter 6).

Write to All the Companies

Whether or not you apply via e-mail or online, you should still consider applying by mail to the vast

FIGURE 7.2 Mystery Shopping Companies' E-mail Addresses

A Closer Look	E-mail: info@closer-look.com
Audits & Surveys Worldwide (Cybershoppers)	E-mail: mshoppers@surveys.com
Courtesy Counts, Inc.	E-mail: www.courtesycounts.com
Customer Perspectives	E-mail: recruiter@customerperspectives.com
Customer's View, Inc.	E-mail: shoppers@customersview.com
Evaluation Systems for Personnel	E-mail: ESPShop@ESPSHOP.Com
Marketing Systems Unlimited, Corp.	E-mail: info@msultd.com
Market Viewpoint	E-mail: info@marketviewpoint.com
National Shopping Service Network	E-mail: howard@mysteryshopper.net
S.G. Marketing Group, Inc.	E-mail: sgm@sgmarketing.com
Sales Builders Marketing, Inc.	E-mail: brewer4@sbmarketing.com
Service Evaluation Concepts	E-mail: feedback@serviceevaluation.com
Service Performance Group, Inc.	E-mail: www.serviceperformancegrp.com
Service Quest	E-mail: tturgeion@dataquestionline.com
Ser-View	E-mail: Ser-View@Ser-View.com
The Locksley Group	E-mail: LGLgroup@aol.com
The Secret Shopper Company	E-mail: recruiters@secretshoppercompany.com
The Shadow Agency	E-mail: shopper@theshaddowagency.com

majority of the companies that do not use computer-based electronic vehicles for shopper applications. As rapidly as possible, it is wise to prepare a form letter tailor-designed to fit you and send that letter to each of the mystery shopping companies listed in chapter 6 of this book. As soon as you get a response, fill out the forms and return the completed forms to each company. The probability is that within two weeks one or more of the companies will call you with an assignment.

Complete that assignment as professionally as possible. Send in the shopping report on time. Wait two or three days and then call or write the person from the company who gave you your first assignment and ask for more assignments. By constantly taking assignments, completing them professionally, filling out the paperwork right away, getting your completed reports to the companies within twenty-four hours of completing the shop, and then calling for more assignments, you will be able to rapidly build the income you want to receive from mystery shopping.

Working for Many Companies Means More Work, More Money, and More Fun

Mystery shoppers who want to earn a good add-on income will work for a number of companies. This means that as companies call with assignments, shoppers can be more selective as to the assignments they accept. By being selective, the money paid for each shop will usually increase due to the fact that shoppers often turn down low-paying assignments, accepting only the higher paying (and usually more enjoyable) assignments. Most mystery shopping companies have a core group of shoppers who work only for them and who will accept any assignment. Company executives know they can give the lower paying, less-enjoyable assignments to these people. Therefore, once you decide to expand beyond the first company that gives you an assignment and you start shopping for several companies, you will find that your income per assignment should increase, the quality of assignments will usually become better, and your total monthly income from mystery shopping may well double or triple.

Expand to Companies Hiring Only Experienced Mystery Shoppers

Once you have "worked" the companies listed in this book, you may be ready to expand further. The next step is to approach companies that hire only experienced mystery shoppers. These companies usually pay much better for each assignment simply because they require experienced shoppers and they know that they will have to pay more to get a shopper who may currently be loyal to only one or a few companies.

If you made phone calls from the Yellow Page telephone books of cities far from where you live in order to add to the number of companies you initially wanted to work for, you probably found that a number of the companies you called told you that they only hire experienced mystery shoppers. Now (after you have completed several mystery shopping assignments) is the time to go back to these companies. Tell the corporate executive you speak to that you are an experienced mystery shopper and offer to share with that executive the name of the company or companies with which you have worked. Then ask for application forms from the company that only hires experienced shoppers.

You may also want to subscribe to *The Mystery Shopper*. In fact, many people subscribe to *The Mystery Shopper* as soon as they start mystery shopping, accumulating the names and contact information for companies that hire experienced mystery shoppers as each new issue comes out. In this way, when they are ready to approach companies that want experienced shoppers, they have a list of companies to contact. Generally, each issue of *The Mystery Shopper* will feature several companies that hire experienced mystery shoppers. Since new mystery shopping companies are created every year, there is really no end to your ability to add to your list of mystery shopping company employers. If you contact each new company as soon as you read about it in *The Mystery Shopper* and if you follow up on a regular basis in accordance with the process detailed in chapter 4, you will find yourself in a continuous expansion mode. To subscribe to *The Mystery Shopper*, turn to the end of this book, fill out the subscription form found there, and send the form together with your check to the address listed on the form. You may also decide to purchase one of the packages that include a subscription to *The Mystery Shopper* and one or more other mystery shopping products. All packages are detailed at the end of this book as well, and, of course, order forms for each package are included.

LIST 77

The ultimate contact list is LIST 77. This list contains the names of seventy-seven of the better mystery shopping companies headquartered in North America. It is updated every six months to make certain that all names, addresses, and shopping information is correct and up-to-date. LIST 77 can also be purchased in conjunction with one or more other mystery shopping products in a package of products described at the end of this book.

Expansion May Include Specialization

As you become more selective in the companies with which you work, you may decide that you want to limit yourself to only one or a few of the specialized types of mystery shopping. Like the man in Texas, you may decide that what you most enjoy doing is eating. It won't be hard to specialize in shopping restaurants. You might find that you enjoy comparison price shopping. If you live in a major city, you may find that there is more than enough work in this specialization to keep you busy. Many people like to stay in hotels. Some mystery shoppers make hotel shops a specialty. If you travel a lot, this could be a lucrative specialization.

It is suggested that you not form opinions prematurely. There are many types of mystery shopping. After you have experienced a wide variety of shopping for several months, then decide what specialties you want to pursue. You may be surprised to learn that you enjoy some types of shopping that, before conducting these shops, you would never have thought would be so much fun (and profitable).

Other Directions

While most mystery shoppers concentrate on building their employer base of mystery shopping companies, specializing, and steadily increasing their income per minute by taking the better-paying mystery shopping assignments and passing on those that pay less, some experienced shoppers move in another direction. Some will take on work that is closely related to mystery shopping, and many who do so find that this gives them the variety and the income they seek. The direction in which the second largest number of mystery shoppers move, however, is to start their own mystery shopping company. We will discuss this approach in chapter 8.

STARTING YOUR OWN MYSTERY SHOPPING COMPANY

A Logical Process

One way of expanding is to start your own mystery shopping company. It can be a small, local company serving only neighborhood shops—and this is usually the best way to start. Or, it can grow to become a company that sells its mystery shopping services to businesses that have branch stores throughout your city or in a multicounty area.

The next expansion might be to a slightly larger geographic area. Your shopping company might start serving client firms located throughout a single state (in a large state such as Alaska or Texas) or a single province/territory (in a populated province such as Quebec). You might grow your firm until it is a regional mystery shopping company in an area where there are many smaller states (such as New England). Traditionally, statewide, province-wide, or multistate is the next expansion process after a mystery shopping firm serves a multicounty area.

A few mystery shopping companies will ultimately expand to cover a large region of the country (southeastern Canada, the western states of the U.S., and so forth). Or, you might eventually grow your company to become one that covers all of Canada, the entire United States, or even all of North America.

Only the larger of the mystery shopping companies take on client companies that want a large (countrywide or North America-wide) geographical coverage. Typically, these are clients that have branches or stores in every state, province, and territory. They may be the international fast food chains or the large department stores that have a location in every city of 300,000 people or more. Some mystery shopping companies are international in their coverage. Although there is currently no mystery shopping company with representation in forty or more countries in the world, there are a growing number that offer mystery shopping services to their clients throughout North America and a few serve clients in multiple countries outside North America.

Start Small

Starting small is the way most mystery shoppers get into offering shopping services to client companies—and thereby starting their own mystery shopping companies. Donna Hargrave of Houston is a good example. After several years of experience as a mystery shopper, Donna spoke about the benefits of mystery shopping to a restaurant owner in her neighborhood.

He asked her if she knew of someone who would shop his fine dining establishment. Without thinking, Donna said, "I will." She then realized that she was starting a new career in mystery shopping. At first, she had second thoughts, but then realized that she had shopped fine dining restaurants a lot since becoming a mystery shopper. In fact, fine dining was her favorite kind of mystery shopping. She knew what fine dining restaurant owners wanted, and she practically knew by heart the kind of questions asked on fine dining shopping reports.

Donna put together a letter of agreement spelling out the number of shops that would be conducted, the number of mystery shoppers she would use (herself, her husband, her daughter, a friend, and other mystery shoppers she knew), and a fee based on the total number of shops that would be conducted during the initial contract.

Together Donna and the restaurant owner worked out a shopping report. He knew the problem areas he wanted to have checked, but based on her experience in mystery shopping a large number of restaurants, Donna was able to suggest additional concerns that might be considered—such as the restaurant's valet parking service.

As Donna's mystery shoppers visited the restaurant, the owner found that he was able to increase both the quality of service and the quality of the food that was served. The outstanding quality built an increasingly better reputation for the restaurant. The reputation of the restaurant produced more clients and more repeat visits from patrons. The increase in visits resulted in increased profits. The owner was (and remains) happy with the services of Donna's mystery shopping company, and he has recommended Donna's company to other retailers.

Donna now has three local clients. All are fine dining restaurants. None are chains. Although Donna realizes that she could make much more money with multiunit retailers, she has chosen not to expand. She realizes that more work would be needed if she contracted to provide mystery shopping outside of Houston and with mystery shoppers outside the circle of her family, friends, and the mystery shoppers she knows. One day she may decide to expand, but for now Donna says that this sideline from being a mystery shopper is just right. Her small company is profitable, and it requires little additional work on her part. Some day Donna may become what she describes as a "full-fledged" mystery shopping company, but she started small and for now she is happy staying small.

Growing Your Own Mystery Shopping Company

Most mystery shoppers who expand into having their own mystery shopping company do it the way Donna did. And, most elect to stay small. However, much more money can be made if the company becomes regional or offers either a national or an international geographic coverage to its clients. One contract from a key executive at the client company's headquarters can result in payment to provide a large number of shops. The profits from a single regional coverage contract or a national coverage contract can result in profits many times what Donna is able to earn each month.

But an expansion to regional, national, or international coverage requires both more marketing and finding a large number of mystery shoppers. It usually means having at least one person working full-time calling on potential client companies. Initially, at least, that one person is the owner—you. And if you don't like or are not good at selling, you won't enjoy the job and you probably will not be successful at it.

Finding Mystery Shoppers For Your Company

One of the biggest problems in growing a mystery shopping company is finding mystery shoppers who will do a good job while working at a compensation level that will still allow the company to make a reasonable profit. Since at least one mystery shopper must be found in each location where the client firm has a store, branch, or affiliate, a large number of mystery shoppers are needed—and often they must be found over a large geographical distance.

One approach to finding mystery shoppers is to contact the author/publisher of *The Mystery Shopper*. In your letter, identify the region of the country (give the name of each state or province/territory) where you need mystery shoppers; provide the postal codes of these areas. The names and addresses of mystery shoppers who are subscribers to *The Mystery Shopper* who reside in the postal code areas you list are provided to mystery shopping companies on a gratis basis. Even the cost of reproducing the list and mailing it to you will be picked up by the author/publisher of *The Mystery Shopper*. A number of mystery shopping companies, some of them quite large in geographical coverage, have used this free service. It benefits both the shopper and the mystery shopping company.

Another approach is to place a want ad in local newspapers. Although this approach is used, the quality and the reliability of mystery shoppers found in this way tend not to be as good as you might want. Classified advertisements are costly, and one runs the risk that too few qualified people will respond to the advertisements.

Starting Your Secret Shopping Business

By Judith Rappold

One of the best sources for the person who is serious about starting a mystery shopping company is a book by Judith Rappold, CEO of Business Resources–Mystery Shopping in Austin, Texas, called *Starting Your Secret Shopping Business.* The book originated as a compilation of materials from Rappold's three-day seminar of the same name. It was reissued in a completely updated fourth edition in September 2001. This book is aimed at persons who have been shoppers and would like to expand and have shoppers working for them. In the mystery shopping business for about fourteen years, Judith originally specialized in local and regional mystery shopping. About five years ago, she moved into serving national accounts. Fortunately, this is reflected in her book.

The twelve sections in Judith's approximately four hundred-page book cover the field. Chapter titles include: Getting Set Up, Marketing Your Services, Targeting Specific Customers, Preparing Secret Shoppers,

Tracking Work in the Office, Evaluating Shoppers' Reports, Designing Report Formats, Statistical Reporting, Other Services You Can Offer Customers, Pricing Your Service, Managing Finances, Ethics and Success.

Special features of the book include fifty pages of report format examples for many varied kinds of businesses—everything from beauty salons, retail stores, and supermarkets to car repair shops and government agencies. It contains considerable information on marketing your company, including sample press releases. Proposal samples range from a one-page proposal for a local company wanting a few quick, easy shops to lengthy multipage proposals for national and international chains wanting each store shopped on a weekly or monthly basis. The book also includes a sample of a proposal for a government agency.

Section 6 of the manual includes benchmarks for judging the quality of shopper reports, guidelines on how to spot problem reports, and suggestions on what to do when receiving reports that do not meet the standards of your company or your client.

Getting customers is one of the most daunting tasks new mystery shopping companies face. Section 3 is worth the price of the book for its suggestions on how to market your new business.

Published in a large 8.5-inch-by-11-inch format, the approximately two-inch thick book sells for $599 plus $15 for shipping and handling. If you would like to receive more information about the book, call Judith at (512) 416-7702 or check out her Web site at www.buzpublications.com. To order the book, call the same number and give Judith your Visa or MasterCard number and related data. Alternatively, you may send her a check for $614. Make the check out to: Business Resources–Publications and mail it to 2222 Western Trails Boulevard, Suite 107, Austin, Texas 78745. Your third option is to fax an order to Judith at (512) 416-7732. On the fax order, be sure to include your credit card information and the address to which you would like to have the book sent.

The Step-by-Step Hand-Holding Option

The author of this book, *Mystery Shopping*, and the quarterly newsletter for mystery shoppers, *The Mystery Shopper*, Jim Poynter, has honed a process over the years to help those who have been working as mystery shoppers to start a home-based, locally oriented mystery shopping company. These are companies that can be operated from one's home on a part-time basis. The process allows shoppers to continue to mystery shop for major national companies while simultaneously getting their shopping company underway. By starting a small, local mystery shopping company these shoppers are able to generate a steady flow of additional income, build a business that can one day be sold by a business broker for a surprisingly large sum, and provide diversity in the source of income earned each month. It also positions the new mystery shopping company so that it can usually be expanded into a regional, national, or multinational shopping company at a later time if those who own it wish to do so. In other words, your mystery shopping business can be structured to be exactly what you want it to be—large or small.

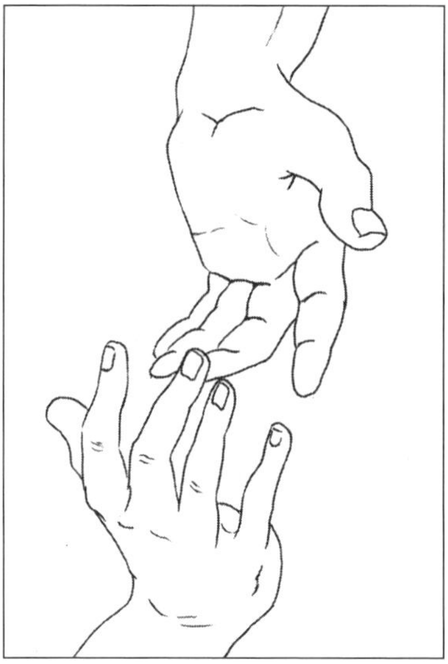

The key with this approach is to take it step-by-step. If you elect to subscribe to this program, each month you will be asked to undertake some local research, review and make changes to forms, and/or to make a few local phone calls. The program is designed so that within a year you should have your own tailor-designed mystery shopping company. In addition, you should have customers, a business plan, an operating plan, and a recognized cadre of mystery shoppers briefed and ready to shop your local clients. In fact, if you follow the step-by-step approach, within a year you should have a start-up mystery shopping company that is in business, operating, and providing income for you.

Like other worthwhile new company consulting, there is a cost involved. But the cost may be less than you would think. The reason is that the process has been streamlined. It is essentially the same process that has been used with others who have started their mystery shopping companies in locations throughout the country. Business plans for shopping companies of a wide variety of types have been prepared. Typically, people who want to start mystery shopping companies pay far more for start-up consulting services because the typical consultant who specializes in business plans works with many kinds of companies. Each one is a business start-up unique to itself. Each plan requires considerable thought and consideration. In addition, the consultant often winds up doing (and being paid to do) much of what the owner could have done at a much lower cost. With this program, however, you will be doing the local (expensive to farm out) research work. And you will not have to pay for the expensive analysis costs. You will be shown how to do that part yourself.

Of course, it should be kept in mind that starting a new business is never easy. Starting a local mystery shopping service will involve work as well. However, because with this consulting program the work will be spread out over a one-year period, the amount of work needed in any one single month will be minimal. In a typical month a person starting a mystery shopping company utilizing this program can expect to put in between ten and twenty hours of effort building his or her mystery shopping business. This work will involve starting and building a business plan; getting a local and/or state business license; filing a name for your business with the proper authorities; preparing a marketing plan; designing basic operating documents; finding, selling, and briefing appropriate mystery shopping retail clients; finding and briefing a cadre of mystery shoppers; and a few other necessary tasks. You will be guided in a logical, progressive pattern every step of the way. Although most of your work will involve carrying out routine, easy-to-understand tasks, some of your undertakings will be harder. By following the step-by-step process, however, you will move your mystery shopping company from the nucleus of an idea into an increasingly sophisticated local mystery shopping service.

Competition is a concern. Although most cities are home to few mystery shopping companies, based on their population a small number of cities in North America already host a large number of mystery shopping companies. No one can control competition, so there is no way to make certain that you will face little or no competition. However, other local firms that want to offer mystery shopping services will usually be operating in the blind. They will rarely have the advantage of working with a consultant who has a history of successfully helping to set up local mystery shopping companies or a consultant who has the wide range of mystery shopping company contacts that your consultant enjoys. And since it is unethical for a consultant to simultaneously provide the same services to directly competing companies, you can be certain that you will not be going head to head with another new mystery shopping company that is getting the same advice from the same consultant in the same geographical area.

The fee structure is unique. It allows you to discontinue the start-up consulting services at any time you wish to do so. There is a start-up fee of $300 and then payments of decreasing amount are required every two months for a year. Altogether the total amounts to a reasonable $1,194 for a year of consulting services. Any time you feel you are ready to go it alone, just stop sending the bimonthly consulting fee. Termination is just that easy.

In addition to the consulting fee, of course, you will have some local phone calls to make, forms to process and reproduce, and a small amount of postage. For most people who work the business out of their homes, the total start-up costs run far lower than those for the average start-up company. Keep in mind that after the first several months of operation you should be able to sell your mystery shopping company through a business broker for many times your total investment. In fact, some start local mystery shopping companies specifically with that in mind. In approximately eighteen months of business, most mystery shopping companies can sell for multiples of at least four times their actual investment costs. But you probably won't want to sell. The steady monthly checks you receive as a result of your company providing shopping services for local client firms will be a strong incentive to let the income just keep flowing in month after month.

To get started, make the decision that you want a local mystery shopping service of your own. Once that decision is made, fill out the Registration Data and Statement of Agreement form at the end of this chapter. Make out a check to Jim Poynter for $300 and be sure to show that it is for local mystery shopping company consulting services. Send your completed and signed Registration Data and Statement of Agreement and your check to Jim Poynter at Post Office Box

40484, Denver, Colorado 80204. Within two weeks, you will receive your first package of materials and set of forms to complete in order to get your new local mystery shopping company off the ground.

A Combination of Approaches

Consultants, books, service organizations, and other individuals and businesses exist to help you succeed in your efforts to start a profitable mystery shopping company. It is suggested that you use them as you need them. You might want to start by making an effort to do it all on your own. You will soon discover whether or not you are comfortable doing it all on your own. If not, it is suggested that you start with the consulting service package offered by Jim Poynter. As you move forward, ask yourself each month if you really need his services. As soon as you feel comfortable that you can go it alone, discontinue his services.

Next, you might want to turn to Judith Rappold's book. Buy it. Review it. And based on her book, revise your mystery shopping company determining whether or not each piece "fits." By working with each one of the "helping" sources in the areas where that organization/firm specializes, your chances for success will be magnified.

Figure 8.1 Start-up Mystery Shopping Company Consulting Services Registration Data and Statement of Agreement

(Please Print or Type)

(Mr.) (Ms.) (Mrs.) Name: (Last) ________ (First) ______________

Address ____

____

Phones:

Home ____

Office ____

Other ____

Date Day of Week: _______ Month: ___ Day: ___ Year: _______

STATEMENT OF UNDERSTANDING

I understand that Jim Poynter will provide consulting services for me on an ongoing basis as I undertake starting a retail oriented mystery shopping service in my local area. I understand that Jim Poynter will not simultaneously provide consulting services to mystery shopping services headquartered in an area within twenty-one miles of my home. For his consulting services, I am including a $300 check for start-up fees. I will mail additional checks to Jim Poynter over a one-year period on the dates determined by the following formula below and in the amounts indicated in the following formula: sixty days from today, $249; one hundred and twenty days from today, $199; one hundred and eighty days from today, $149; two hundred and forty days from today, $99; three hundred days from today, $99; and three hundred and sixty days from today, $99. In exchange for these payments in his role as a consultant, at a minimum, Jim Poynter will help me to: 1) sign up customers, 2) develop a tailor-designed business plan, 3) create an operating plan for my company, and 4) line up local mystery shoppers. I understand that I may terminate the agreement to contract for mystery shopping consulting services at any time by simply not making the next due payments, but that Jim Poynter will cease to provide local company mystery shopping company consulting services if and when my payments are ceased.

______________________________ ______________________________

Name Printed Name Signed

______________________________ ______________________________

Name of Witness Printed Name or Witness Signed

CHAPTER 9

RELATED JOBS

A Wide Range of Related Opportunities

For those who have gained experience as mystery shoppers, a large number of other, related jobs are often available based on their mystery shopping experience. The three where there is the greatest demand are:

1. Training in the form of focus groups.
2. Field representative work.
3. Private detective investigative work.

However, mystery shoppers are often employed to do market research in the form of exit interviews with customers (and noncustomers) who are leaving (exiting) stores, advertising signage reporting work (describing store signage and other both in-store and out-of-store advertising), comparison price checks (sometimes called price audits), and various types of other jobs. For most mystery shoppers, these "related opportunities" are exactly that—jobs that sometimes come their way and are loosely related to their work as mystery shoppers. However, some mystery shoppers find themselves doing these "related" jobs more often than mystery shopping, and some mystery shoppers ultimately find themselves making more money in these "related" jobs than from their jobs as mystery shoppers.

Private Detective Investigative Work

Work that involves gathering information in which either the data gathered or the process used in getting the information involves legal issues and/or risk will frequently be contracted to private investigative services. For example, some firms that want theft control checks done for them will contract to have it done by a private detective (investigative) service rather than a mystery shopping company. These agencies/services also contract for people to perform employee theft checks of all types as well as for a wide range of other "observational" types of work (spotting shoplifters, for example).

Because the observational skills needed for much of this work is similar to or the same as those skills honed by mystery shoppers, experienced mystery shoppers are frequently employed by the companies wanting these services. In most states, however, state licensing laws must be met, and the majority of the detective agencies and investigative services will do a background check on the mystery shopper before offering employment. These background checks are

usually to establish the shopper's financial credibility, but many will also check to see that the applicant does not have any criminal history. Keep in mind that the key skill the shopper is marketing is the ability to observe detail without being noticed—the ability to gather needed data while being totally obscure and in such a way that no one will ever remember the shopper. Experienced shoppers learn how to do this quite effectively. To be good at it is marketable.

Price Comparison Checks

If you have shopped much, you have probably noticed people with paper and pen in hand going over each item on a store shelf noting model numbers, brand names, and item prices. These are price comparison

shoppers. For many years, retailers have known that they can sell merchandise if they promise to offer clients the lowest prices in town. We have all heard or read the advertisements that say the firm will meet or beat the price of any competitor in town. Most of the time, they promise that if the customer will bring in a sales slip or other proof of an item being less expensive elsewhere, they will give the customer the difference. If the retailer provides this guarantee and does not follow through, potentially expensive legal action may be brought against the store. It is time consuming and expensive for a retailer to constantly make refunds to clients. Therefore, companies that claim to have the lowest prices will often employ the services of mystery shopping companies and other firms that provide price comparison checks.

Many customers compare prices before buying. Some of them bring paper and pen with them and jot down information in each store to make sure they are comparing prices on the same brands and the same models. Store managers know this, and therefore, store managers usually tolerate it. However, when the store employees see a person going down the aisle checking the price of each item, noting model names and manufacturer for each item on the shelf, they know they are dealing with a person who is paid to do price comparison checks. Store managers are usually far less tolerant with these individuals, and it is not unusual for these people to be asked to leave the store.

Experienced mystery shoppers constitute some of the best price comparison checkers. They have usually done some comparison shopping for mystery shopping companies. However, comparison shopping assignments usually involve buying one or two items at up to three stores, and most of the time mystery shoppers are expected to report on service, display conditions, how well the shelves are stocked, and other areas of importance in addition to price.

Nevertheless, most mystery shoppers have gained experience in shopping retailers, and they have learned how to blend in and how to gather data without being noticed. Experienced mystery shoppers rapidly learn to come back to the store two or three times at different times of the day and different days of the week. They will often go to other departments from time to time, returning to the one where they are gathering information once or twice during a store visit. They will usually visit the store's restroom at least once during their visit to a store—where they will jot down information. Some are adept at wearing a tape recorder and mumbling to themselves. Many will come in with friends and verbally discuss the pros and cons of a product and its prices—all the while tape recording what they are saying to one another. But experienced mystery shoppers will never take out a pad of paper and pen and start writing down information while in a merchandise aisle. Their ability to get the data while remaining confidential is why they are so valuable to their employers and to the clients of their employers. Firms that specialize in (and often only do) comparison price checks, therefore, like to employ experienced mystery shoppers—especially those mystery shoppers who have done a number of comparison shopping assignments.

Focus Groups

Participating in focus groups constitutes one of the more enjoyable add-ons for experienced mystery shoppers. Many shopping companies offer feedback to their client company executives through the vehicle of a focus group. Therefore, you will not necessarily need to work for a new company when you become a paid member of a focus group. In most cases, you will be doing *additional work* for a current mystery shopping employer.

Typically, a panel of two or more mystery shoppers discusses the pros and cons of the client company's stores and service compared to the client's competitors. Since mystery shoppers see everything from the point

of view of a shopper, not an employee, their comments are usually insightful.

Some focus groups are local, and some are regional in nature. The client company, a department store, for example, will bring in the various department heads for the focus group training meeting. Typically, three or four experienced mystery shoppers will have completed shopping assignments in three or more departments of one store in the client's chain of stores. These same experienced mystery shoppers will have completed shopping assignments in the same departments of between two and four competing stores in the same area of town as the client's store is located.

Each shopper keeps a copy of his or her shopping

reports—both for the client's store and for the competing stores. Each of the department heads also has a set of the shopping reports. The focus group starts with each shopper explaining what he or she found to be the pros and the cons of the client company's store compared to each of the competing stores. Price and service are two of the more important issues, but typically the shoppers will address store merchandise presentation, ease of finding items for which they were shopping, store lighting, how fast they were helped, how cordial store employees were, whether or not department managers seemed to be present, and so forth.

After shoppers present the pros and cons, department managers candidly discuss the findings. Usually the moderator attempts to identify patterns and frequently the moderator/coordinator will identify a range of "profitability" goals based on the findings of the mystery shoppers. Many focus groups are scheduled over lunch or dinner in a store's training room, and the atmosphere is purposely kept informal. There is usually an easy give and take between the shoppers who are presenting their findings and the department managers who are considering the change recommendations that frequently come out of focus group training sessions.

Most mystery shoppers find focus group participation a welcome change of pace and a beneficial additional income source. Shopping companies typically pay shoppers $30 to $75 to participate in a focus group panel. This, of course, is on top of the pay they receive for conducting usually a minimum of three shopping assignments in preparation for the focus group training.

Field Representative Work

Working as a field representative for a mystery shopping company can be lucrative. In addition, it is a logical extension to mystery shopping employment. Field representatives are employees of the mystery shopping company's home office, but they reside in and work in their local city and state. There are two types of field representative employment. The most common is sales. The field representative is expected to call on potential accounts and convince those accounts to use the services of the mystery shopping company. Typically, the field representative is considered a salesperson for the company and is paid a commission on each contract sold. Although a few mystery shopping companies hire full-time field representatives as salespersons, it is far more common to hire on a part-time basis. This allows the company to get the benefit of having a local contact person, but not have the overhead involved in employing a full-time person. Sales have to generate enough income to justify the payment of benefits. Some companies will move a part-time, commission-only field representative into a full-time salaried position with a sales quota once the sales volume justifies such a move. The next step, but one taken by few mystery shopping companies, is to move the field representative from a full-time salaried position with a sales quota to a full-time salary with sales quota plus a bonus for sales exceeding the quota.

Whatever the compensation arrangement, however, it should be kept in mind that most mystery shopping companies that hire field representatives for sales want individuals with a substantial amount of mystery shopping work experience. And, most of these companies prefer to hire shoppers who have worked for their company for quite some time. Persons with substantial experience as shoppers with a firm know the requirements of a company. They know the company's policies and the likes and dislikes of the firm's executives. Perhaps most importantly, they know the mystery shopping company's set of standards and can feel comfortable in talking with potential customers about the level of service and the types of service that will be provided. After all, they speak from experience.

In spite of the fact that mystery shopping firms seek shoppers with substantial experience with their company, it is wise to stress that you would like to work your way into a field sales rep position with the firm when you first apply to be a shopper with them. Some companies will hire you as a shopper in order to groom you for the position of sales field rep. Other companies may suddenly find that they need a sales field rep in your area. Knowing of your interest, they may contact you for the position much earlier than they otherwise would have.

It is hard to find good salespeople. If you have a history of successful sales, the chances are good that a national or regional mystery shopping company will be interested in working with you once you have a solid history of mystery shopping.

The second type of field representative is the person who is asked to line up mystery shoppers in his or her region for shopping assignments. When mystery shopping company executives find that they have a large number of contracts in an area some distance from their headquarters office, they frequently decide that it will be less expensive and more expeditious to hire someone locally to line up shoppers and coordinate client shopping visits. Typically, they will offer this type of position to an experienced mystery shopper residing in the area. Usually this type of field representative position starts out being part-time. However, if the field representative does a good job and if the volume of shops the company contracts to do in the area continues to grow, it is not unusual for the part-time shopping coordinator field representative to be offered full-time employment.

In this position, too, experienced mystery shoppers are the persons company executives prefer to hire. After all, an experienced shopper is a person who knows the company and who knows what is involved in undertaking shopping assignments. In addition, some local mystery shoppers know other local mystery shoppers and are often in a better position to find someone to cover a shopping assignment at the last minute in case of last-minute cancellations.

Here, too, it is best to let company executives know of your interest in the position as soon as you decide that you would like to undertake shopper coordination field representative work. Of course, if you are interested in undertaking both sales and shopper coordination—and you let the mystery shopping company executives with whom you work know of your dual field representative work interest—your chances of getting a phone call asking you to take on field representative work will be much greater.

Exit Interviews

Some shoppers love doing exit interviews; others hate it. But exit interviews are a way of providing multiple shopper opinions to a client at a low cost per shopper opinion. Typically, mystery shoppers will be expected to undertake a shopping assignment in the same way as they normally undertake shopping assignments. However, after leaving a store, instead of going back to his or her car, making notes, and going home to complete the shopping report, the shopper will be asked to interview four or five shoppers exiting the store before leaving the parking lot.

Normally, mystery shoppers interview few exiting shoppers (five at most), and they ask only a few questions. They may go up to a person who is leaving the store and, after briefly explaining that they are conducting an exit interview, ask the shopper if anything was purchased. If so, they ask why the shopper purchased the item at the store and whether or not they enjoyed their buying experience. The mystery shopper jots down responses. If the exiting shopper did not buy anything, the person is asked if they will explain why. Again, the information is noted. After getting this type of information from five exiting shoppers, the mystery shopper leaves and prepares his or her shopping report in the same way he or she would prepare a shopping report for any shopping assignment. However, the mystery shopper also prepares reports on the four or five exiting shoppers interviewed. The interview reports, of course, are briefer and less detailed than a normal mystery shopping report.

The mystery shopper is paid for conducting the shop and writing a report about his or her shopping experience. But the mystery shopper is also paid for talking with four or five exiting shoppers and writing reports about what they said. Everybody wins. The mystery shopper earns substantially more (sometimes twice the income per shopping assignment). The mystery shopping company earns income from providing two shopping feedback services for its client company. The client company gets reports about the shopping experience of five or six clients or potential clients, instead of just the one report normally received. And the client company gets the additional reports at a bargain price per report.

Advertising Signage Reports

One of the easiest add-on jobs for mystery shoppers is advertising checks. Many major companies spend a substantial amount of money on signs. Some of these will be posted in their stores—encouraging clients to buy more products or more expensive products. Other signs will be on the exterior—encouraging would-be clients to come in and shop. A good example of companies that utilize advertising checks are oil change firms. Exterior signs exhort clients to come in and get their oil changed in a minimum amount of time. Interior signs identify a number of additional services customers may purchase while getting an oil change.

In advertising and signage checks, mystery shoppers report what signs appear outside the building and what signs are posted for customers to see inside the building. The headquarters office wants to know that the substantial amount of money it spent in preparing signage advertising has not been wasted by employees simply putting the signs in a back room (or throwing them away). Typically, a shopper will be asked to report monthly regarding what signs can be seen as one drives by the store. These, appropriately, are called "drive by" signs. In addition, they will be asked to stop in the store at least once every three months and report on what signs are posted inside.

Although the pay for advertising and signage checks tends to be low, most shoppers find that if they accept assignments for undertaking these checks in locations that are on their way to and from work or other places where they drive frequently, it is an easy way to add a few dollars to their income without requiring more than a few minutes of their time each year.

Who Are the Employers and How Do You Get the Job?

Fortunately, the employers are frequently the same ones you are already working for—mystery shopping companies. For jobs such as focus group participation, exit interviews, field representative work, and advertising/signage reporting and for many of the price comparison check jobs, all you have to do is tell your contact at the mystery shopping company that you would like to work for the company undertaking these types of assignments if the company has such work in your area. Just letting mystery shopping company executives know that you want to take on this type of work is often all you need to do. If and when they have such assignments in your area, you will get a call. But except for field representative work, don't ask until you have experience with the company as a mystery shopper. After you have successfully completed five or six mystery shopping assignments with the firm and its executives know that they can count on you to do a quality job in a timely manner, telling the person who next calls you with a shopping assignment that you would like to work for the company in its related areas of client sales and service will initiate the process that should give you several additional, financially rewarding assignments.

Other work involves contacting other employers. Although some mystery shopping companies are also private investigative services, the majority of detective agencies (and private investigation services) are not affiliated with mystery shopping companies. For work with these companies, start by contacting local firms. Turn to the Yellow Pages listing for the phone numbers of companies in your city. The section where you will find the listings of interest to you will be under the heading of "Investigators." These agencies tend to specialize. Most do no work that will require the services of mystery shoppers. A few specialize in such services, and many more will do some work involving mystery shopping (or related) work from time to time. One approach is to send a letter to all companies listed and follow up on your letters with a phone call indicating your interest in working with the company. Alternatively, you might read through the listings (and Yellow Page advertising), identify those firms most likely to need your services, and send a letter to each of these companies. Again, you will probably get more assignments if you follow up with a phone call a few days after company executives get your letter. When you review the listings of investigative services, it is likely that you will find some that advertise that they will provide mystery shopping services for potential clients. While these are the companies that will be more likely to hire you, they are few in number in any metropolitan area. Generally speaking, you will be better off contacting all the companies in the listing and following up by phone.

Most of the companies that undertake price comparison checks are mystery shopping firms. However, other companies provide this type of service for client retailers as well. In addition to approaching mystery shopping companies for this type of work, try contacting companies that list themselves in the Yellow Pages under the categories of "Market Research and Analysis" and "Marketing Consultants." By far, the majority of the firms listed in these two categories will not offer price comparison checks as a service for their clients. However, some of them will offer such a service. These are the companies that will be more likely to hire you. Here, too, the best approach is to send a letter to all firms listed under the two categories in the Yellow Pages for your hometown. It is also best to follow up on your letter with a phone call a few days after your letter should have arrived in the mail.

By actively seeking add-on work, you will be surprised at how rapidly you will be able to get additional assignments. The nice thing is that most of the add-on work can be done during hours when you are not working at your full-time job. You will have multiple employers, not just one. And, like with mystery shopping, it is okay to say "no" if they call you with an assignment you would rather pass on.

CHAPTER 10

THE TEN-STEP PROCESS FOR MAKING TOP MONEY

Yes, You Can Make "Real" Money

Compensation levels were discussed in chapter 2. It was clearly pointed out that a person working as a part-time mystery shopper undertaking a few assignments a month for one mystery shopping company will not bring home a substantial amount of money as a mystery shopper. However, those who set goals, work for a large number of companies, specialize in high-paying assignments, and constantly work at earning top money as a mystery shopper are usually able to ultimately get to the point where they are bringing in incomes of $2,000 to a little over $3,000 a month as mystery shoppers. It is rare for a shopper to make as little as $100 a month, and it is even more rare for a person to make as much as $3,000 a month. However, the range between these two extremes is rather large.

Since many people really do want to work steadily toward maximizing the income that can be attained from mystery shopping and related work, this chapter provides a step-by-step guide to starting as a mystery shopper, moving into earning a "good" monthly income as a mystery shopper ($800 to $1,000), and finally moving into the ranks of the best paid mystery shoppers. Although a large number of people—perhaps even the majority of those who ultimately get the best incomes from mystery shopping—do not follow these steps in exactly the same way they are set out here, those who do follow the steps the way they are presented tend to be successful. But there is no magic formula. If you would prefer to skip a couple of steps and then go back to them later, feel free to do so. We encourage you to read each step, consider it, and then devise a plan that you personally are comfortable with. What works well for one person will not necessarily work equally well for another. However, if after considering each of the steps, you set out a plan that you believe will work for you, the chances are you will be able to move yourself fairly smoothly from one income level to the next. And, if you consistently move forward step by step, the chances are good that you will soon reach a point where you will be bringing in the amount of money that you want to earn as a mystery shopper—and you will be doing it while maintaining a comfort level that will allow you to continue to do it over a long period of time.

STEP ONE

The first step is to get a first mystery shopping assignment as rapidly as possible. For psychological reasons, it is important to get a first assignment right away. Otherwise, you, like most people, are likely to lose interest in mystery shopping, stop working toward getting assignments, and give up on making the kind of money and having the kind of fun mystery shopping can provide for you.

Since getting a first assignment rapidly is the first step, it is suggested that you concentrate on Internet opportunities. Turn to chapter 7 and review the section on "Computer-Based Mystery Shopping Companies." Set aside some time and apply with all shopping companies that provide assignments via the Internet (either those with a Web site or those with an e-mail address).

STEP TWO

Next, apply to all companies listed in this book. Write to them requesting employment as a mystery shopper. As soon as you get forms from them in the mail, fill in the forms completely and accurately. Return them right away. When you do this, you should be well on your way to getting a steady flow of mystery shopping assignments.

STEP THREE

Set up a system for applying with companies that prefer to work with experienced mystery shoppers. Go back to those you contacted from your telephone book research where a company executive said the firm only hires experienced shoppers. Subscribe to *The Mystery Shopper.* Write to each company featured in each issue as soon as you receive an issue. Also write to each company not already contacted from your telephone book research. You will find that not only will the volume of your mystery shopping assignments pick up dramatically, but also that your average pay per assignment will increase substantially.

STEP FOUR

Create a regular follow-up system. Establish a tickler file and contact each company for which you are not working every six weeks reminding them that you would like to work with them on assignments in your area.

STEP FIVE

Make it a policy to always ask for multiple assignments every time you talk with a mystery shopping company executive. When an assignment is offered to you, whether you take it or not, always follow up with the question, "What else do you have?" You will be amazed at how often you will come away with multiple assignments.

STEP SIX

Contact local mystery shopping companies. After working with several national or international mystery shopping firms, turn to the local and regional mystery shopping companies based in your city. Write asking for shopping assignments—and be sure to emphasize that you have experience with some of the best national or international mystery shopping companies. Again, set up a tickler (follow-up) file on these local and regional mystery shopping companies and follow up with those that do not give you assignments right away.

STEP SEVEN

Specialize in the high pay assignments. With each company for which you work, after completing a few assignments, ask the person who calls you with jobs what the highest paying assignments are that the company has in your area. Then ask what you have to do to be able to get these high pay assignments. In some cases, it will be as simple as just asking for them.

STEP EIGHT

Start a small mystery shopping company of your own. Contract with just one retailer (a local restaurant will usually be your best bet) to perform a shop once a week, twice a month, or once a month. After you become comfortable in serving this one client, consider taking on one or two additional local retailers as clients.

STEP NINE

Add a "related" job. Try your hand at private detective investigative work or being a member of focus groups. Alternatively, you might try doing exit interviews, advertising signage reporting work, or price comparison checks. It is not suggested that you try all of these at the same time. Decide which ones you think you would like to do and try the one you like the best for a while. Stick with it if you like it over a period of several months. Add others from time to time until you have a balance of add-on jobs that you can turn to for additional money, but drop those efforts that are in areas with which you are uncomfortable or where the income is less per hour than your hourly goal rate.

STEP TEN

If maximizing your income is your goal, follow what successful retailers and moonlighters have done for years. Drop the "lines" (jobs or employers) that pay the least and increase your work with the employers and jobs that pay the most. Mystery shopping and its related endeavors offer so much work and such a wide range of work that those who continue to market themselves, monitor what they are paid per hour, and follow a strict policy of continually increasing their work with the highest paying employers and jobs, frequently and rapidly find themselves in the enviable position of making several times more than the average mystery shopper—and having a lot more fun making top dollar.

INDEX

I

J

L

M

MYSTERY SHOPPING COMPANIES EXPERIENCED SHOPPER NEWSLETTER

Every three months North America's shopping newsletter, *The Mystery Shopper*, is published for experienced mystery shoppers. This publication is for persons who have completed at least one shopping assignment for a mystery shopping company. Most subscribers are people wanting to add to the list of companies for which they work as mystery shoppers. Since some mystery shopping companies only want to employ experienced mystery shoppers, those companies, contact information for those companies, and mystery shopping assignment information relating to those companies does not appear in the book, *Mystery Shopping*. For the most part, these are considered the **best paying** mystery shopping companies and the **only place they are listed** is in the quarterly mystery shopping companies experienced shopper newsletter, *The Mystery Shopper.*

In addition to listing several **new** mystery shopping companies in each issue of the newsletter, helpful hints are included in articles that are geared toward helping you do a better, faster, and more profitable job of mystery shopping. **And,** *The Mystery Shopper* also serves as a company information update vehicle. When there are new contact persons, new addresses, new phone numbers, or when companies provide any information that is new and that will assist our readers to get more work as mystery shoppers, make their jobs easier, or provide them with an ability to do a better job, that information is included in *The Mystery Shopper.*

The Mystery Shopper is sent to subscribers four times a year usually during the last week of March, June, and September and during the December/January holiday period. To subscribe, complete the form on the next page and attach your check for $19.95 (U.S.) or $37 (Canadian) made out to Jim Poynter. Send both to: **Jim Poynter, P.O. Box 40484, Denver, CO 80204.**

MYSTERY SHOPPING COMPANIES
EXPERIENCED SHOPPER NEWSLETTER

PLEASE PRINT

Your Name: ______________________________

Your Address: ______________________________

City: ________________ State: _____ Zip: ____________

Your Phone Numbers: Home ______________________

Work ______________________

Be sure to attach your check for $19.95 (U.S.) or
$37 (Canadian) made out to Jim Poynter.

Your phone numbers are optional and are requested only so that they may be given to mystery shopping companies that ask for contact information for mystery shoppers residing in an area where they are looking for shoppers. If you do not want mystery shopping companies to call you at your home or your place of work, please leave the phone number lines blank.

THE 77 MASTER LIST KIT

EVERYTHING you need to apply. Not only do you receive the most complete and up-to-date listing of major regional, national, and international mystery shopping companies, but this listing meets the needs of the mystery shopper who wants to make top money fast. Updated every three months, the list not only identifies the name and current contact information for each of seventy-seven mystery shopping companies that hire mystery shoppers, it also identifies shopping specializations, territories covered, and where available, income ranges.

EASY AND SIMPLE! Yes, with the components you get, it is both easy and simple to apply. For companies that prefer to be contacted by mail, we have prepared peel-off labels. Just prepare a modified version of the application letter reproduced in your book. Then use one set of the labels for letter headers to each mystery shopping company and the other set of labels for the envelopes. Some companies prefer that mystery shopper applicants contact them by e-mail or by going directly to their home pages to apply online. For these companies, we have made application easy as well. You will receive a CD-ROM disk that includes all the e-mail addresses and all the home page addresses of those companies that prefer electronic applications. Just put the disk into your computer's CD-ROM player and work your way through the e-mail addresses that come up. When you have finished that, go to the home page address file and work your way through applications on one home page after another. The 77 List makes it as simple as possible. If you are like most who use it, you will be able to make application to all seventy-seven companies in a few hours the day you get the 77 List Package.

FOLLOW-UP is also important. In addition to all of the above, you will receive one hundred follow-up forms. Just fill one out for each company that does not respond to your initial contact and start a follow-up (tickler) file. Every six weeks send a reminder to the company until you have employment with them.

THE MYSTERY SHOPPING AUDIO AND VIDEO PROGRAMS

The Mystery Shopping Seminar audiotapes and videotapes are compilations of several of Jim Poynter's mystery shopping seminars that were taped "live." The tapes have been professionally spliced and edited to make sure you get all of Jim's professional advice, hear and/or see all of his examples, and learn all of his success tidbits. You even see and/or hear the audience chuckle when Jim's award-winning and entertaining stories point out examples of "how tos" and "how not tos." If you don't want to take notes during one of Jim's mystery shopping presentations or if you missed his seminar, but still want to attend, one or both of these tapes are for you. The cost of the audiotape is just $14 (U.S.) or $21 (Canadian) including shipping. The cost of the videotape is only slightly more: $20 (U. S.) or $29 (Canadian). Simply fill out the form on the back of this page to order Jim's Mystery Shopping Seminar Audiotape or his Mystery Shopping Seminar Videotape.

THE MYSTERY SHOPPING AUDIO AND VIDEO PROGRAMS

PLEASE PRINT

Your Name: ______________________________

Your Address: ______________________________

City: ______________ State ______ Zip ______________

Your Phone Numbers: Home ______________________

Work ______________________

PLEASE CHECK THE ITEM(S) YOU WISH TO ORDER

_____ Mystery Shopping Audiotape

_____ Mystery Shopping Videotape

_____ Both the Mystery Shopping Audiotape and the Mystery Shopping Videotape

Be sure to attach your check for $14 (U.S.) or $21 (Canadian) for the audiotape; $20 (U.S.) or $29 (Canadian) for the videotape; or $32 (U.S.) or $45 (Canadian) for both the audio and the videotapes. Please make your check out to Jim Poynter and send the completed form and the check to P. O. Box 40484, Denver, CO 80204.

THE MYSTERY SHOPPING MLM PROGRAM

Offering one of the fastest and least expensive ways of getting into mystery shopping *and* multilevel marketing, this $5 (U.S.) or $8 (Canadian) program introduces the novice to mystery shopping and multilevel marketing. In addition to the initial $5 (U.S.) or $8 (Canadian) investment, there are five additional $5 (U.S.) or $8 (Canadian) payments required for a total investment cost of a little over $30 (U.S.) or $48 (Canadian). Suggested only for those who own their own in-home computer with access to the Internet. Most who follow the program find that they can get their entire investment back plus ongoing incomes from the Mystery Shopping MLM Program. It includes the names and contact numbers of ten mystery shopping companies.

MLM programs work when they offer quality products at bargain prices. That is exactly what the Mystery Shopping MLM Program offers—a great product at an even better price. But they also need solid referrals. Before investing in this program, it is suggested that you take out a pen or pencil and paper and write down the names of ten people (friends and/or family members) who you believe would really like to become mystery shoppers and who would invest $30 (U.S.) or $48 (Canadian) to do so. If you cannot think of ten people, please do not order the Mystery Shopping MLM Program. If you can think of and you are able to list ten, please fill out the following application for the program.

THE MYSTERY SHOPPING MLM PROGRAM

PLEASE PRINT

Your Name: ______________________________

Your Address: ______________________________

City: ________________ State ______ Zip ______________

Your Phone Numbers: Home ____________________

Work ____________________

Be sure to attach your check for $5 (U.S.) or $8 (Canadian).

PACKAGES

PACKAGE ONE: A full year's subscription to the newsletter, *The Mystery Shopper,* the Mystery Shopping Seminar Audiotape, and the Mystery Shopping MLM Program. The cost for the package is $30 (U.S.) or $54 (Canadian). This represents a savings of $8.95 (U.S.) or $12 (Canadian).

PACKAGE TWO: A full year's subscription to the newsletter, *The Mystery Shopper*, the Mystery Shopping Seminar Videotape, and the Mystery Shopping MLM Program. The cost for the package is $34 (U.S.) or $60 (Canadian). This represents a savings of $10.95 (U.S.) or $14 (Canadian).

PACKAGE THREE: A full two-year subscription to the newsletter, *The Mystery Shopper*, the Mystery Shopping Seminar Audiotape, the Mystery Shopping Seminar Videotape, the Mystery Shopping MLM Program, and the 77 Master Kit. The cost for the package is $99 (U.S.) or $170 (Canadian). This represents a savings of $34.90 (U.S.) or $40 (Canadian).

PACKAGES ORDER FORM

PLEASE PRINT

Your Name: ______________________________

Your Address: ______________________________

City: ______________ State ______ Zip ______________

Your Phone Numbers: Home ______________________

Work ______________________

PLEASE CHECK WHICH PACKAGE YOU WISH TO ORDER

_____ Package One

_____ Package Two

_____ Package Three

Be sure to attach your check for $30 (U.S.) or $54 (Canadian) for package one; $34 (U.S.) or $60 (Canadian) for package two; or $99 (U.S.) or $170 (Canadian) for package three. Please make your check out to Jim Poynter and send the completed form and check to P. O. Box 40484, Denver, CO 80204.